Jack Lenor Larsen
Creator and Collector

Jack Lenor Larsen
Creator and Collector

David Revere McFadden
Mildred Friedman
Lotus Stack
and Jack Lenor Larsen

MERRELL
LONDON · NEW YORK

Foreword and Acknowledgments

It is with a sense of great pleasure and privilege that we honor Jack Lenor Larsen with this exhibition, the first collaboration of the Museum of Arts & Design (formerly the American Craft Museum) and the Liliane and David M. Stewart Program for Modern Design. He has been a vital part of both our institutions since their inceptions.

In 1956, as a board member of the American Craft Council, Jack helped lay the cornerstone of what was then called the Museum of Contemporary Crafts. He served on the board until 2003. In 1996 the Council gave him its Gold Medal, and in 2000 the Museum of Arts & Design honored him with its Lifetime Achievement Award. Throughout his career, he has donated important examples of twentieth-century design and handcraft, as well as his own textiles, to the museum. And, more important, the constant gifts of his wisdom and expertise have widened and enriched our institution.

Jack was a founding member of the Montreal Museum of Decorative Arts (MMDA) Collections Advisory Board, and he served the museum assiduously—the first in North America dedicated solely to twentieth-century design—throughout its lifetime. In 1981 he began giving exemplary modern designs to the MMDA. In 1982 the museum hosted the major traveling exhibition *Jack Lenor Larsen: 30 Years of Creative Textiles*, and in 1987 he donated an archive of his own work, including some eight hundred samples of his textiles. In 1999 he was recognized by the museum with its third annual Design Arts Award. He continues to act as consultant to the Stewart Program for Modern Design on acquisitions for its collection of contemporary crafts, design, and decorative arts, and he remains a trusted adviser and beloved friend.

Jack's relations with the Museum of Arts & Design and the Stewart Program typify the collegial spirit we share with one another. In his generosity with his expertise and time, Jack set a standard few board members can match. His career epitomizes our mandates: both the museum and the Stewart Program represent the best examples of twentieth-century design, from the limited-edition handcraft to the industrial product.

Fig. 2. **A bay window** at LongHouse with a collection of glass vessel forms, most by Dale Chihuly

Larsen's creative eye and to inform his constantly evolving designs. They have fluid boundaries and often overlap in his fabric designs and in his collections; and there are, of course, other design issues and concepts embedded in his œuvre. Nonetheless, we believe that the exploration of these five themes through the works Larsen has collected and those he has created will lead viewers to appreciate the intricate and subtle nature of the creative process more fully.

Jack Lenor Larsen received his MFA from the Cranbrook Academy of Art with fiber as his medium, but he did not study design in any formal sense. To this day, he refers to himself as a "weaver" and a "servant to architecture,"[3] having been enamored of building from his early childhood. Indeed, he views this subject as fundamental to his developing eye as a designer and his skill as a weaver. Through his examination of architecture he gained a deep understanding of the importance of controlling natural light in any structure, using the maximum to illuminate interiors and open them to the

Fig. 3. **A light-filled seating area** in the living room, LongHouse

environment, or the minimum to allow the occupants privacy and assure their comfort. The "Larsen Look" was created, to a great extent, by the designer's innovative experiments with sheer or reflective fabrics utilizing an understated palette of natural, neutrally hued fibers: they were a perfect complement to the spare and restrained simplicity of modern architecture.

As a practicing weaver and Modernist designer, Larsen conducted his trend-setting experiments with materials and techniques to produce surfaces and textures that animated interiors and furnishings with tactile appeal.

As a colorist and avid student of world cultures, he used hue and pattern to seduce and delight the viewer. Through color he expressed another facet of his vision, looking far afield to exotic parts of the world and to distant times, to the history of art, and to his beloved gardens for inspiration. Color and pattern became, for Larsen, a second language.

Larsen describes his creative trajectory as bringing together "the aesthetics of architecture, the color of painting, and the techniques of weaving."[4] These

concerns are reflected in his perennial experiments with the subtleties of surface and texture and in his passionate interest in the architectural forms and structures of past and present. His global wanderings, which have taken him to most countries and to every continent, have given him unique opportunities to study architecture and design in their original contexts. In his two major building projects on Long Island— Round House and LongHouse—he brought two examples of that architecture home.

Round House was inspired by the graceful and generous circular forms of the Bantu dwellings he saw on one of his early trips to Africa, in 1960. For Larsen, the circular form of the structure fulfills the practical responsibilities of a weekend house and expresses his social philosophy. Round House, he wrote, "was intended as a simple shelter from the elements, for those hours when my friends and I could not be out-of-doors. Walled spaces between the round house, guest house, and studio would become outdoor rooms, creating a more intriguing composition than that of most small houses."[5] Radically different in form, but equally compelling in design and function, is Larsen's masterwork, LongHouse, situated on sixteen acres of land in East Hampton. LongHouse's imposing shape (an articulated rectangle 180 feet [55 meters] in length supported on elegant pillars) appears to float above the ground, hovering over the intelligently planned and lavishly planted gardens. The design is based on the seventh-century Shinto shrine that Larsen encountered on a visit to Ise, Japan.

If form and structure are the core of his overall design approach, they have also shaped his eye as a collector. For Larsen, the bones of any design are as meaningful as the skin, whether they be in a building, a ceramic vessel, or a piece of wooden furniture. He has always been attracted to the strength and discipline of pure geometric forms. In sculptural objects, however, his predilection has, more often than not, veered toward more organic and sensuous forms, as seen in the curvilinear basketry he has chosen, in the spirited natural shapes of ancient and prehistoric pottery, and in the elegant and curvaceous profiles of hand-raised silver.

Today the Larsen collections are a cross-section of world expressions. They include rare objects from distant or vanished cultures and from parts of the globe that boast strong and vital folk traditions, as well as a stellar group of works created by artists—famous and emerging, young and old—exploring craft media today. The sympathies that have shaped the singular vision of Larsen the designer and Larsen the collector can be best appreciated in viewing a selection of his fabric designs in conjunction with these objects: the treasured, essential accoutrements that have most pleased Larsen's eyes and hands. They help one to understand the reasons for his success in designing the diverse fabrics sampled here. Fabrics are probably the most body-focused of all media; we wear them from infancy to death; we use them for protection, shelter, and comfort, and to express our individuality; they provide tactile and visual pleasure on a daily basis. The crafts of world cultures are equally intertwined with the lives of their makers and owners.[6]

Fig. 4. **The winter living room**, LongHouse, with some of its collection of modern American furniture design

[1] "Art and Morality" in *Phoenix: The Posthumous Papers of D.H. Lawrence*, ed. E.D. McDonald, New York (Viking) 1936, p. 525.

[2] Jack Lenor Larsen, quoted in *Conference of American Craftsmen, June 12–14, 1957: Asilomar, Calif.*, New York (American Craftsman's Council) 1957, p. 37.

[3] Unless otherwise cited, statements by Larsen were gathered during a series of interviews with the author between fall 2001 and spring 2003.

[4] *Industrial Design*, 2, 1955, p. 11.

[5] Jack Lenor Larsen, *Jack Lenor Larsen: A Weaver's Memoir*, New York (Harry N. Abrams) 1988, p. 103. See also "Round House Revisited: Jack Lenor Larsen's Country House in East Hampton, Long Island," *Interior Design*, 56 (April 1985), pp. 210–15. Larsen's fascination with the craft and design of sub-Saharan Africa began early in his career; see "African Motifs Interpreted by Jack Lenor Larsen in His Newest Fabrics," *Handweaver & Craftsman*, Spring 1963, pp. 6–7, 41.

[6] "I concluded that for most of us collecting would be a manner of focusing on the special and unique, often subsidized by exclusion of normal necessities. Art that was useful, even on occasion, was particularly valued." Larsen, *A Weaver's Memoir*, p. 136. See also David Masello, "Grand Larsen-Y," *Art & Antiques*, September 2001, pp. 77–83. Larsen's attitude toward collecting has always embraced the drama and theatricality of display: "I've always wanted a living environment with the flexibility of a stage," he told John Allen; "Props for a Personal Theater: Jack Lenor Larsen's Craft Collection," *American Craft*, February/March 1980, p. 17.

The Ambassador-at-Large

Mildred Friedman

Fig. 1. **View of Lever House**, New York, designed by Skidmore, Owings & Merrill, 1951–52

Fig. 2. **Jack Lenor Larsen**, detail of curtain fragment for the lobby of Lever House, New York, *c*. 1952. Linen and Lurex; lace weave. New York, Collection Cowtan & Tout

Jack Lenor Larsen was a Depression-era child, raised in a time when America was essentially isolated from the rest of the world. But when a family friend in Seattle presented that small boy with a world map, a globe, an atlas, and albums for postage stamps, what would become an enduring interest in geography and history began. And in the 1950s, when the post-war world was opening up to jet travel, Larsen, by then a college graduate, began his remarkable journeys to some of its most exotic places. In that regard, he believes that Americans are a hearty people on the move, who have more in common with tribal peoples than with the courtly Europeans most often cited as their exemplars.[1] Perhaps this belief helps explain his wanderlust and his well-earned role as a world citizen, and as an unofficial arts ambassador-at-large.

In many remote areas of the world, Larsen found weavers with whom, despite the lack of a common spoken language, he had astonishing rapport. They used exotic materials in unusual ways and readily shared their knowledge and talents with a fellow weaver who understood their work. On his travels,

Larsen learned about materials, forms, and working methods unknown in America. His understanding of these far-flung aesthetics and his ability to adapt aspects of them to modern textiles give him a unique place in the evolution of twentieth-century design.

Modernism at Mid-Century

Beginning his career in New York City in 1951, Larsen immediately contributed to the world of Modernist architecture and "Good Design." Even though he had not yet traveled outside the United States, he saw that hand-woven, custom-designed textiles could soften the polished, sleek interiors of contemporary buildings. His first important commission was the design of a lobby drapery for Skidmore, Owings & Merrill's Lever House (1951–52) (figs. 1, 2). Here his translucent fabric was used to divide the interior space, and it modulated the light with its weave, which incorporated metallic yarn. The wide media attention given to Lever House, one of the first International Style buildings in the United States, also put a spotlight on Larsen, then just twenty-five years

old. Within a year, he had established Jack Lenor Larsen, incorporated [*sic*], soon including in the firm his school friend Win Anderson and Bob Carr, a weaver from Los Angeles. It was an exhilarating time to be a designer in the United States.

Larsen was welcomed by an older generation of pioneering architects and designers who were buoyed by America's prosperity at mid-century. Designs by Charles and Ray Eames and George Nelson, with fabrics by Alexander Girard, were being put into production (and so given wide attention) by Herman Miller, the adventurous manufacturer of domestic and office furniture. At the high end of the market, Knoll, Dunbar, and Risom were among the furniture manufacturers promoting the aesthetics that Larsen's work exemplified. The Museum of Modern Art and the Walker Art Center were two of the institutions supporting the work of such architects as Edward Larrabee Barnes, Charles Moore, Eero Saarinen, and Bernard Rudofsky, the sculptor-designer Isamu Noguchi, and the designers Alvin Lustig, Harry Bertoia, Eva Zeisel, Russel Wright, Gyorgy Kepes, and Paul

Fig. 3. **Dorothy Liebes**, prototype theater curtain for Dupont Pavilion, New York World's Fair, 1964. Orlon and Fairtex metallic yarn; power-loomed. New York, Museum of Arts & Design, Gift of Dorothy Liebes Design

Fig. 4. **Anni Albers**, *Tikal*, 1958. Cotton. New York, Museum of Arts & Design

Rand. Among the older generation, Frank Lloyd Wright (who would use Larsen fabrics at Taliesin, his Wisconsin home and school) and Marcel Breuer were still unflagging forces in architecture and the debate about its direction. Contemporary architecture and its interior design accoutrements were also publicized in a variety of periodicals in those years, including *House Beautiful*, *House & Garden*, and *Interiors*. While, for the most part, Middle America remained resolutely traditional and uncomfortable with change, exceptions could be found in the Mid-Atlantic states, on the West Coast, and among the participants in the Case Study House program in Southern California initiated by the California-based magazine *Arts & Architecture*. These efforts, in addition to introducing the work of a number of young architects, helped open the door to textiles that were designed to create appropriate backgrounds and supporting elements for the new interiors. The advocates for this new design were vocal, if relatively few. They applauded Larsen's talent, energy, and eloquence, and would find him an able liaison between art and industry.

Influential Weavers

Many of the older generation of architects and designers were world citizens—émigrés from Europe who had introduced avant-garde design concepts to America in the 1930s and 1940s. Many of them also taught in American schools of art and architecture, thus exposing an eager new generation, which included Larsen, to challenging aesthetic disciplines. Among those influential émigrés were, first, Richard Neutra and Eliel Saarinen, and then Mies van der Rohe, Walter Gropius, Marcel Breuer, and the great weaver Anni Albers, who had studied and taught at the Bauhaus in Germany. With her husband, the painter Josef Albers, Anni moved to the United States in 1933, to live and teach at Black Mountain College in North Carolina. In 1949 they moved to New York City where she was the first textile designer to have a one-person exhibition at the Museum of Modern Art. Devoutly Modernist, her designs were often pure abstractions (fig. 4). She was "the figurehead of the avant-garde" in textiles, Larsen later wrote. "Although she had been involved with the rediscovery of texture, her work of

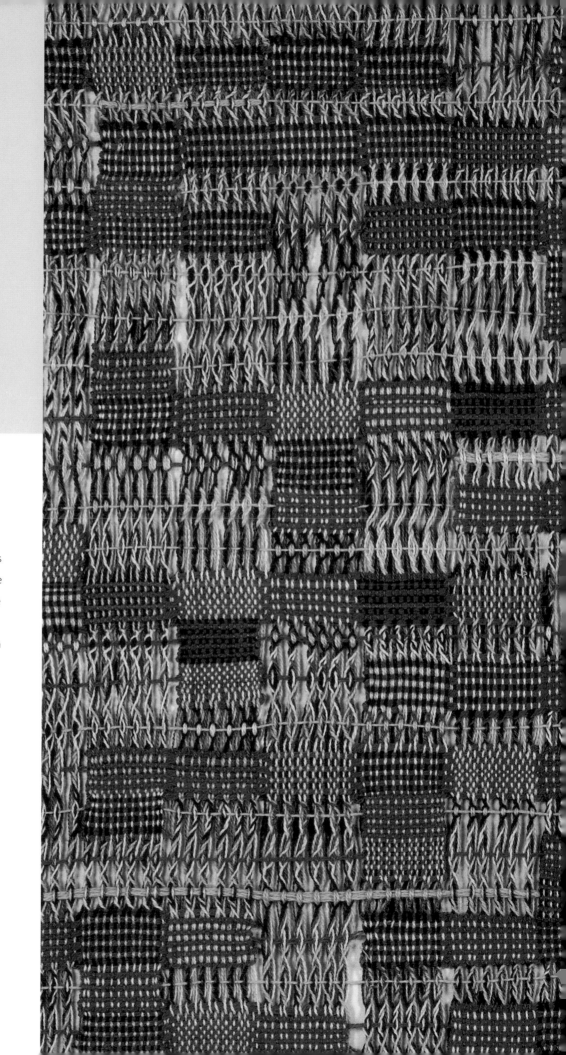

this period . . . [concerned] architectonic pattern. . . . [S]he was the writer and academician insistent upon clear thinking. She also helped to focus our attention on pre-Columbian weaving."[2]

The example of Modernism in weaving set by Albers was not, in fact, a lodestar for the young Larsen. Before he reached New York, he had admired the work of the celebrated weaver Dorothy Liebes, as well as that of Ed Rossbach and Marianne Strengell. Larsen had begun his college education in the School of Architecture at the University of Washington, Seattle. But during the summer of 1948, while in Los Angeles, he determined that he was not a "drawer," as he put it, but a weaver. Weaving cloth is immediately rewarding, Larsen says, a solo act—rather like painting—while architecture is a slow, deliberate process that requires interaction with clients and contractors. In the late 1940s he had visited the redoubtable Dorothy Liebes in her San Francisco studio. Assuming that Larsen was seeking a job, she asked to see his samples. When he laid out a long strip of small woven squares, she said, "Oh, what a wonderful stripe! But I'm sorry. You won't fit in my

Fig. 5. **Ed Rossbach,** textile, 1960. Polyethylene, cotton; plaited, tie-dyed, discharged. New York, Museum of Arts & Design, Gift of Daphne and Peter Farago

studio—there is only one designer here." She was at that time, according to Larsen, the most influential textile designer in the United States, experimenting with unusual materials as the basic elements of her vividly colorful expression (fig. 3). As he wrote, Liebes "introduced over-scaled textures in finger-thick yarns and reinvented, in her own terms, window blinds of heavy slats supported on warps striped with shimmering contrasts of matte and shiny, rough and smooth, and above all, flamboyantly colored materials."[3] She adapted hand-woven prototypes to the power loom when she became a consultant to industry, as Larsen would do later.

While at the University of Washington, Larsen also met the weaver Ed Rossbach, who had recently graduated from the famed Cranbrook Academy of Art and would become renowned for his inventive weaving techniques and his writings on basketry and other ancient textile methodologies (figs. 5, 6). Rossbach invited Larsen to be his teaching assistant, a post the student held for three semesters. The next logical step for Larsen was graduate work at

Cranbrook, where he hoped to earn the degree that would qualify him to teach at college level. Once enrolled at Cranbrook, however, he chose instead to concentrate on his weaving skills, spending endless hours at his loom. Larsen's "weave master" at Cranbrook was Marianne Strengell from Finland, whose innovative approach to the loom influenced generations of young weavers. Her strength as a designer included the development of textiles using man-made fibers for such applications as automobiles and airplanes. As a teacher, she was also a severe taskmaster. Larsen recalls her saying to him early on, "Jack, I'm disappointed in you." "Why?" he asked uncomprehendingly, "I work *very* hard." Her stern response was, "As you're the only one on scholarship, I expect much more from you." After that admonition, Larsen soon began to gain speed and greater efficiency at the loom. And, although he had gone to Cranbrook in order to become a professor, the formidable Strengell demonstrated to him that being a textile designer was an enticing alternative.

In the tradition of Liebes and Strengell, one of

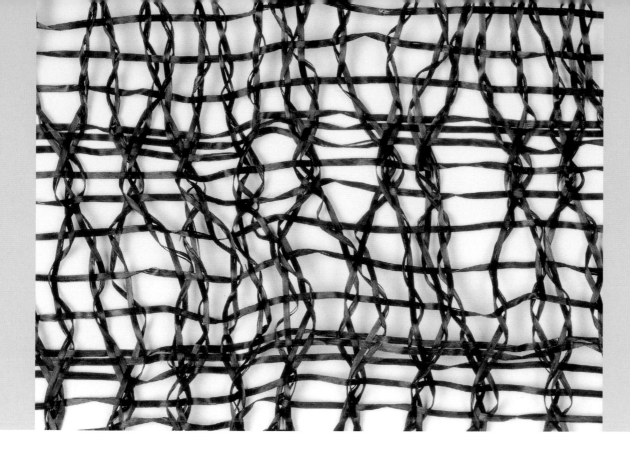

Fig. 6. **Ed Rossbach**, *Casement*, 1948. Rayon straw; double twining. Brooklyn Museum of Art, Gift of Jack Lenor Larsen

Larsen's most important contributions to textile design history has been his ability to take weaving from hand-craft to the realm of commerce. As he puts it, "A power loom is simply a hand loom with a motor attached to it. If you feed it the same material the results will be exactly the same." At the same time, he also came to the conclusion that "the great loss of the industrial revolution was not hand-weaving, but hand-spinning."

It was the hand-spinning of ungraded fibers that impressed Larsen when he made his first trip to Haiti in 1952, the year he established his company. From Haiti and then Morocco, Colombia, and Mexico, he began importing hand-spun hand-weaves that he adapted for the American market. Not long thereafter, through their mutual friend Edgar Kaufmann, Jr., Larsen met Alexander Girard, then director of textile design at the Herman Miller Furniture Company. Both men were showing their work in the Museum of Modern Art's *Good Design* exhibitions organized by Kaufmann, who was director of the museum's design department from 1946 to 1955. Later, Girard engaged Larsen to create fabrics for the celebrated house designed by

the architect Eero Saarinen in the 1950s for the Cummins Engine Company's chief executive, J. Irwin Miller, in Columbus, Indiana (fig. 7). Eero, the son of the distinguished Finnish architect Eliel Saarinen, expanded on his father's example, bringing an elegant, expressive Modernism to his buildings and his furniture designs. The human scale and open planning of the Miller house, built between 1953 and 1957, were given added warmth by the hand-woven look of Larsen's textiles. At the same time, his supremely functional fabric designs harmonized with Saarinen's unpolished marble walls and the other elements of the architect's spare, geometric aesthetic.

In addition to their work with textiles, Girard and Larsen shared an interest in collecting vernacular crafts and folk art. Today, over 100,000 objects based on Girard's collections reside in the Museum of International Folk Art in Santa Fe, New Mexico, while Larsen's vast assembly of extraordinary works is on view at LongHouse, his home on the east end of Long Island. Larsen, who began collecting while still in college, remembers that his teachers and mentors

Fig. 7. **J. Irwin Miller House**, Columbus, Indiana, designed by Eero Saarinen, 1953–57, with interiors by Alexander Girard. View of living area and conversation pit showing fabrics by Larsen.

Fig. 8. **Mark Tobey**, *Autumn Fields*, 1957. Tempera on paper, 47 × 36 in. (119.4 × 91.5 cm). Washington, D.C., Smithsonian American Museum of Art, Gift of S.C. Johnson & Son, Inc.

were ardent acquisitors. To acquire was not to amass quaint souvenirs, in the view of Larsen and Girard, but to find design inspirations and cross-cultural kinships in an era hungering for international understanding.

Exotic Aesthetics

In the early 1950s Larsen was identified with natural fibers and a palette of corresponding neutrals. One of his favorite colors was khaki. In the years following World War II, this hue with its military associations was definitely not a design trend, but Larsen refused to abandon it. In mid-decade the furniture manufacturer Knoll Associates paid tribute to the designer by replacing its primary-colored fabric collection with his earthy palette. It prominently featured khaki (and mustard).

This reticent palette, so suitable for richly textured woven cloths, was not Larsen's only interest, however. In the mid-1950s he began branching out into printed fabrics in more saturated hues, and by the end of the decade had pioneered the technique of hand-printing on velvet. Indeed, though he has always been best

known as a weaver, many of the textiles manufactured by Jack Lenor Larsen, incorporated, were printed. Most often these are the work of designers in his studio. Larsen's travels and friendships—always crucial to his creativity—supported this direction, which anticipated the high-voltage palettes generally associated with the 1960s.

As for patterns, the market's most familiar ones in the mid-1950s were, in Larsen's words, "usually simple or simplistic, often with Swedish influence."[4] His friend Girard espoused brilliant colors in hard-edged flat patterns, and gave printed fabrics architectonic structure through the repetition of abstract, geometric forms.[5] Girard was primarily an interior architect and a gifted print designer, not a weaver. Larsen himself explored a more complex idiom in his prints from the late 1950s and, toward the end of the decade, he supported Edward Wormley and Edgar Kaufmann in their revival of Art Nouveau and Tiffany glass.[6] Larsen's affinity for the decorative subtlety of the *fin-de-siècle* style can also be seen in some of the glass and metalwork art objects he would later collect.

Fig. 9. **Round House**, East Hampton, New York, designed by Jack Lenor Larsen and Robert Rosenberg, 1960–64

Another of Larsen's aesthetic quests led him to an association with the charismatic Jim Thompson, for he recognized the brilliant color sense of this quiet American designer-architect. In 1960 Larsen renewed an early acquaintance with Thompson when he was working in Saigon with the designer Russel Wright, under the auspices of the US Department of State. The two were part of an effort to make local handcrafts suitable for export, a mission intended to encourage the Asians to resist the blandishments of Communism by providing jobs and foreign exchange. In Thailand, Larsen spent weekends with Thompson, who had founded the Thai Silk Company with headquarters in Bangkok, and the two became friends. Thompson urged Larsen to start a company in Burma similar to Thai Silk. Although Larsen loved Burma, and was prepared to stay in Asia, the Communist government of Thailand was soon expelling all Westerners. Thompson, who had lived in Bangkok for many years, remained, but in the late 1960s he mysteriously disappeared and, tragically, was never found. A few years later, Larsen purchased Thaibok

Ltd., the Thai Silk Company's American franchise, which became a part of the Larsen firm. He has designed in Thailand ever since, introducing new weaves and yarns, ikats, and, more recently, hand-crafted sheer casement fabrics.

The electric hues of Siamese pink, chartreuse, and the like suited the vibrant tastes of the 1960s and helped to mold them. But Larsen could also draw on other aesthetic experiences. His upbringing in Seattle, so different from that of his European contemporaries, was a major influence on the work of this world traveler. Notwithstanding his eventual departure for New York, the Pacific Northwest embodied memories for Larsen that, as an adult, he continued to find inspiring. He loved the saltwater bays and the green-misted landscape, so evocative, he thought, of Japan, where he would later spend a great deal of time. The palette typical of the region's art at mid-century—understated, lyrical, close-toned—appealed to him. And it was in Seattle, when he was at the University of Washington, that he began his long friendship with the legendary

Mark Tobey, who evoked the magic of the Northwest landscape in his elegant "white paintings" (fig. 8). Morris Graves was another painter in the area whom Larsen knew and admired. All three were influenced by Asian calligraphy and by the enigmatic landscape of their region.

In 1965, Larsen met another Seattle artist, Dale Chihuly, who would become one of his lifelong friends (and a subject of his collecting). Like Larsen, Chihuly had entered the University of Washington to study architecture and then changed his major to weaving, but he eventually became a pioneering artist whose sole medium would be glass. In the same way that Larsen revolutionized Western textiles through his work abroad, Chihuly's Pilchuck Glass School, established with Larsen's encouragement in 1971 in Stanwood, Washington, has transformed the way in which that medium is viewed by artists today. Larsen proudly observes that only three Americans have had solo exhibitions in Paris's Musée des Arts Décoratifs at the Palais du Louvre. All are from Seattle: Mark Tobey, Dale Chihuly, and himself.

LongHouse

In Larsen's design and collecting, the Pacific aesthetic, so to speak, has been most fully realized in yet another of his creative pursuits: the architecture and landscape design of his second country home. The sixteen-acre estate, now known as LongHouse Reserve (fig. 11), was designed by Larsen and the architect Charles Forberg in the late 1980s. Larsen's inspiration was the seventh-century Shinto shrine complex of Ise, just south of Nagoya in Japan. Like the allusions to distant cultures of some of his textile designs, LongHouse's references are respectful and synthesizing, without Post-modern irony or obvious historicizing quotations. The sacred places of Japan, a country he began visiting in 1959, are touchstones for Larsen in their serene union of architecture, art, and nature. LongHouse, with its sculpture gardens, arboretum, and gallery, became a foundation in 1991, open to the public five months a year with changing exhibitions of art, performances, and demonstrations within its walls and memorable landscape. Successions of contemporary sculpture have been exhibited there, including commanding ceramics

Fig. 10. **Small ceramics** from a dozen cultures and two millennia in the LongHouse dining room

Fig. 11. **LongHouse**, East Hampton, New York, designed by Charles Forberg with Jack Lenor Larsen, completed 1992. View of the west wing

by Peter Voulkos and Toshiko Takeazu and luminous, fantastic glass sculptures by Dale Chihuly (fig. 12).

The LongHouse gardens themselves are Larsen's creations and reflect his delight in landscaping, which he pursued from the 1960s, as well as the unity of his vision from textiles to plants. He plays down the importance of blossoms, for example, and instead comments at length on the subtleties in the coloration of the leaves and branches that form the basic garden elements. It is the fundamental structures of the gardens that are of particular interest, just as it is the structures of woven textiles that continue to fascinate him. He notes that gardens, like textiles, are constantly in motion, in growth and decline. At this stage of his life, Larsen is acquiring more trees and plants than textiles and objects, although he recently admitted to the purchase of two hundred fabrics in Asia. He bought these, he says, to enrich the archive of ethnographic fabrics at LongHouse: he intends it to become a resource for textile designers and historians,[7] just as the gardens are meant not simply for the public but for students at all levels of landscape design.

Gardening absorbed Larsen from childhood, when he was preoccupied with making things grow. He recalls being given a packet of radish seeds at the unlikely age of three. He sprinkled these onto rows of soil in the backyard of his parents' home, patted them into place, and covered them with cheesecloth. He still remembers his delight at seeing the seeds sprout and watching the plants mature. That was the beginning of his lifelong devotion to gardening. Why didn't he pursue a degree in landscape design? To do so, Larsen says, would have been to go "backwards." His Canadian forebears were wheat ranchers, and he was determined to pursue "more expressive" directions. Thus architecture, interior design, and finally weaving took precedence over landscape design. Nevertheless, LongHouse now challenges his textiles for his attention.

The architecture of the complex is but the latest chapter in Larsen's longtime collaborations with architects, both friends and anonymous builders. (Indeed, his first country home, Round House, was his homage, with the help of architect Robert Rosenberg, to the round structures of the Bantu people of West

Africa; fig. 9.) Larsen has also worked in close association with a number of twentieth-century master builders: not only Eero Saarinen, but also Frank Lloyd Wright, Edward Larrabee Barnes, I.M. Pei, and Louis Kahn. One of the most rewarding of these collaborations was his hiring of Barnes to design the campus of the Haystack Mountain School of Crafts in Deer Isle, Maine. There, Barnes created one of his most restrained, beautifully conceived schemes: a campus of quietly Modernist buildings that has inspired thousands of aspiring designers since its opening in 1960 (fig. 13). Larsen was a force within the school and he long served on its board, as he has on those of the American Craft Council, the Museum of Arts & Design (formerly the American Craft Museum), and the Textile Museum in Washington, D.C., among others.

LongHouse and its gardens are the containers for Larsen's vast collections of fine and applied arts from around the world (fig. 10). What had begun as childhood pursuits—collecting seedlings and postage stamps—expanded during his college days into many other fields. Collecting for Larsen has always been a pleasurable way of exploring the unknown and strengthening his grasp of the world's diverse cultural and technical accomplishments. His collections of textiles at LongHouse, often acquired on his travels abroad, are carefully catalogued and conserved in a system named for Virginia Harvey, a Seattle weaver and textile scholar. Its files will be available to scholars. In addition to textiles, Larsen's acquisitions include a wealth of decorative, artistic, and utilitarian objects— among them the works celebrated in this book and in the exhibition it accompanies. At LongHouse, as in these pages, his collections and his textiles are juxtaposed to underline analogies of form, surface, pattern, and the like. It is here that the strands of Larsen's lifelong creativity and collecting are most fully interwoven.

Though Larsen is revered for his support of artists and artisans worldwide, the authorship of the works he has collected is in some ways less important to him than their originality and the reflections they spark about problem-solving, which he sees as central to creativity. This concept helps explain the rapport with artisans that Larsen has enjoyed over his fifty-year career. His business acumen notwithstanding, he was not especially comfortable working with American industry, although in his early career he was a consultant designer to the giant United States Rubber Company, and to J.P. Stevens, then the world's second largest textile company (after Burlington), for which he designed sheets and jacquard-weave towels (see pl. 102). He much preferred working with weavers from Latin America, Africa, Asia, and with Europeans, where weaving plants were family-owned, with proud traditions. He has had collaborations with artisans in more than sixty countries.

When asked to summarize his achievements in modern textile design, Larsen replies that he believes he has helped restore a sense of craftsmanship to the field, bringing the beauty and character of hand-weaving to more of us. To these contributions should of course be added his own designs, and his introduction to the world market of artisans who live and work in Third World countries. The small hand-weaving centers in Asia and Colombia that have had long-lasting relationships with Larsen's company are typical of his numerous collaborations. Often—but for Larsen—their creativity would be unknown in the wider world. In effect, it is through his unofficial ambassadorial role that Larsen has, over the last fifty years, expanded the breadth and significance of the textile trade, helping to make it global as he has opened our eyes to the wonders of the unfamiliar.

[1] Unless otherwise indicated, Larsen's comments paraphrased in this essay are taken from an interview with the author in August 2002.

[2] Jack Lenor Larsen, "Textiles," in *Design Since 1945*, ed. Kathryn B. Hiesinger and George H. Marcus, Philadelphia (Philadelphia Museum of Art) 1983, p. 175.

[3] *Ibid.*

[4] *Ibid.*, p. 174.

[5] For an essay by Larsen about Girard, written for the 1975 Walker Art Center exhibition catalogue, *The Design Process at Herman Miller*, see *Design Quarterly*, no. 98/99, 1977.

[6] Larsen, "Textiles," p. 175.

[7] A possible inspiration for Larsen's philanthropy is the Calico Textile Museum in Ahmedabad, western India, which he visited in the early 1960s. Established in 1949 by the Sarabhai family, this treasure trove of seventeenth- to twentieth-century fabrics is housed in that textile dynasty's venerable family residence.

Tribute to Jack

Dale Chihuly

Jack Lenor Larsen is an
extraordinary designer, teacher and friend.
He was already a legend when we met
at the University of Washington while
I was still a student in the '60s.
He encouraged me and became a
mentor and introduced me to Harvey
Littleton's glass program in Madison,
where I learned to blow glass.
Later he led me to Anne Gould
Hauberg and John Hauberg which
resulted in the Pilchuck Glass
School. Jack is remarkably
creative and continues to help
artists and craftsmen—opening
doors for them and
helping them find their
way.

Thanks Jack.
Chihuly

Jack Lenor Larsen is an extraordinary designer, teacher & friend. He was already a legend when we met at the University of Washington while I was still a student in the '60s. He encouraged me & became a mentor & introduced me to Harvey Littleton's glass program in Madison, where I learned to blow glass. Later he led me to Anne Gould Hauberg & John Hauberg which resulted in the Pilchuck Glass School. Jack is remarkably creative & continues to help artists & craftsmen - opening doors for them & helping them find their way.

Thanks Jack
Cindy.

014

Tributes to Jack

Edward Larrabee Barnes

JACK LARSEN is a full man—a skilled craftsman, a dedicated educator, an entrepreneur, a museum director, himself a most talented artist, and (to me) a most generous, understanding client. I don't know anyone else who encompasses such a broad range of artistic sensitivity.

The Haystack Mountain School of Crafts has always had understanding directors. Francis and Priscilla Merritt were kind, open-minded, and warm-hearted. But there is no question in my mind that Jack, as leading trustee, had most to do with the selection of the present ravishing site on Deer Isle, Maine, and the move of the school to this incredibly beautiful property. When we planned the school with studios and dwellings stepping down the rocky slope to the shore, it was Jack more than anyone else who understood the significance of this siting. He gave his full support of every move we made as we positioned the studios and cabins on each side of a flight of steps. What an architect cherishes is not just support, but understanding—and Jack, as client, understood from the outset the meaning of the site

with all the buildings free to look straight out to sea.

Now, some years later, Jack's full personality has appeared on Long Island. Here he has created a whole garden world. He has brought forward the best of the location—vistas, groves, glades—and has added garden buildings that truly unify the site. He is, as I have suggested, a Renaissance man—an imaginative promoter and teacher, and at the same time a highly sensitive artist with an eye for art in every form.

Quite separate from all of the above was another brief interlude when my office was doing the "new look" for Pan American World Airways—the logo, the trademark, and the plane interiors. Who should we turn to for fabrics? Jack Larsen, of course. He designed beautiful, tough, sturdy fabrics for all the seats in every class. And he performed this service with efficient business skill and great imagination. The planes would not be the same without him.

I hope this rambling account gives something of a picture of what Jack is all about. And finally, he is and always will be, for Mary and me, a close friend.

Hugh Hardy

JACK LARSEN is a man whose multiple careers represent several lifetimes' worth of accomplishments. A respected leader in numerous branches of the design world, he brings to them the perception, sophistication, and curiosity that inform all he undertakes.

Jack has distinguished himself as a textile designer with the architects Frank Lloyd Wright, Edward Larrabee Barnes, I.M. Pei, Minoru Yamasaki, and with the firm Skidmore, Owings & Merrill. He has designed fabrics for Air Force One, Pan American Airways, and Braniff Airlines. He has worked in sixty countries, many of them in the Third World, adapting their traditions and handicraft skills. Throughout, he has sought innovative uses for materials and manufacturing techniques.

Jack has assembled an unequalled collection of hand-crafted objects at LongHouse in East Hampton, Long Island. He is a patron of young artists, an author (most recently his autobiography, *A Weaver's Memoir*, was published by Abrams), and most splendidly, a garden designer. The LongHouse Reserve sculpture gardens reveal a compelling range of design skills. Here, Jack has shaped the outdoors into many rooms and created many experiences, each knowingly linked to the others. Using a variety of plant species to investigate the subtleties of color, texture, pattern, and transparency, he has created a sequence of magical places.

At first it might appear that all this effort has been a waste, because none of Jack's work can be permanent. Textiles wear out, gardens decay, and the social events for which Jack is famous last only a short time. All are ephemera. But, like the work itself, Jack is concerned with the structure beneath objects, places, and occurrences. His is an exploration of basic generative forms. It is ideas that permeate his efforts, and these will survive, bringing freshness to his designs, prompting us all to observe, to discern, and to demand more of our surroundings. He celebrates the sensual world.

Or, to quote him directly, "I hate repeating myself." "I keep doing something that I don't know how to do yet."

Jack Lenor Larsen's work will continue to challenge and inspire future generations wherever it is discovered.

Design Elements

David Revere McFadden

with textile entries by Lotus Stack

and Jack Lenor Larsen

Light and Translucency

with cords of linen and strands of gold metal were not only revolutionary, but also appropriate."[4]

Larsen says, "without light there is nothing." Inspired by light, he developed a variety of concepts for casement fabrics throughout the 1970s, notably *Chevalier*, 1978 (pl. 12), which features a semi-translucent warp pattern of chevrons. The 1990s saw the introduction of many new patterns that exploited the dynamic relationship between fiber and light. *Nimbus*, 1991 (pl. 8), is a fluffy confection of Saran and polyethylene, heat-treated to shrink, which gives the fabric its cloud-like surface. A related pattern, *Cumulus*, 1991 (pl. 16), continues the cloud motif. Both *Nimbus* and *Cumulus* were spawned by Larsen's lifetime love of nature. In describing their appearance (and feel), he said: "These fabrics look a lot like frost on the windows. As high-tech as they are in their materials and manufacturing techniques, they still look organic and natural."

In *Oberon*, 1969 (pl. 4), Larsen used the "burn-out" or *devoré* technique, a process that involves a heat-responsive acid which, when printed on the fabric, removes passages of the fiber and creates a luxurious pattern of translucency and opacity. *Oberon*, part of the designer's Irish Awakening line, features stylized Celtic spirals inspired by Larsen's travels in Ireland.

Larsen has also been a leader in creating fabrics that respond to the environmental needs for both light and heat control. In 1992 he created *Eclipse* (pl. 11), a solar cloth made of woven polyester that is coated with aluminum powder. The reflective surface thus produced is an effective heat barrier against direct sunlight, yet the weave retains its delicacy and translucency.

The designer has always surrounded himself with objects that exploit different qualities of light, through transparency, translucency, and reflectivity. Larsen was one of the early patrons of a young, talented, and ambitious artist who chose the relatively new field of studio glass as his forte, Dale Chihuly. Chihuly has established his international profile in the field of art glass through his virtuoso handling of the medium, his uninhibited use of color, and his dramatic and memorable installations. Larsen

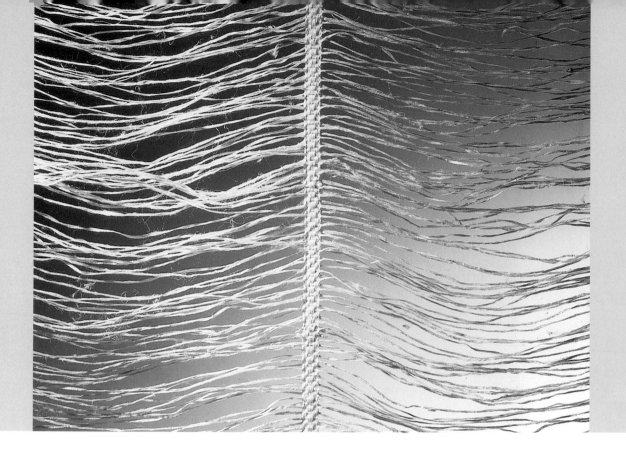

recognized the potential of this emerging star, who began his career as a weaver and came to Larsen's attention as a result of his use of glass strips interwoven with fiber, and his creation of nearly transparent or smoky translucent glass in organic forms that evoke the world of undersea life (pl. 5). On the same aesthetic wavelength in Larsen's collections are works by the brilliant Korean-American metalsmith Chunghi Choo, whose airy *Form in Form, c.* 1980 (pl. 18), captures light in its graceful mesh-wrapped package.

The wearable art of British fiber artist Robin Giddings attracted Larsen's eye with its nearly non-existent structure. He created his *Overgarment,* 1984 (pl. 15), with machine embroidery, stitched in random patterns that look like doodles made with colored pencils. The magic of the design came from Giddings's layering of threads on a soluble synthetic ground that disappeared when soaked in water, leaving behind only the jewel-like stitchery. Larsen also has had a lifelong friend in the gifted textile inventor Jun'ichi Arai of Japan. Arai's work can be

filmy or dense, highly reflective (as in his *Fabric, c.* 1995; pl. 1), or pierced with apertures that welcome light and air. Both Arai and Larsen have taken inspiration from each other and have worked as conspirators in the pursuit of new ways of making light tangible. D.R.McF.

[1] Quoted in Barbara Liebler and Nell Znamierowski, "Interview: Jack Lenor Larsen," *Handwoven,* January/February 1991, p. 18.

[2] Susan Goldin, "Taproot: Jack Lenor Larsen," *Interweave,* Summer 1979, p. 57.

[3] David Masello, "Grand Larsen-Y," *Art & Antiques,* September 2001, p. 82.

[4] Walter McQuade, "One Man's Eden: Jack Lenor Larsen Slowly Weaves a Magic Garden," *Connoisseur,* no. 217, July 1987, p. 102.

Jack Lenor Larsen, *Bahia Blind* (detail of pl. 7)

In the following captions, by Lotus Stack and Jack Lenor Larsen, height precedes width, precedes depth. Measurements are not given for Larsen's textile yardage. The names of countries following those of Larsen's textiles indicate their place of manufacture. For images of Larsen textiles cited in these captions but not illustrated, see the Larsen archives website described on page 185.

OPPOSITE
1. **Jun'ichi Arai** (Japanese, b. 1932)
Fabric, c. 1995
Polyester and aluminum slit film;
shibori-patterned melt-out
379 x 43 in. (965.2 x 109.2 cm) (extended)
New York, Museum of Arts & Design,
Gift of Jack Lenor Larsen

LEFT
2. **Gregory T. Roberts** (American, b. 1968)
Kala Pani, c. 1996
Carved honeycomb clay
26½ x 15 x 15 in.
(67.3 x 38 x 38 cm)
East Hampton, New York,
Collection LongHouse Reserve,
Gift of Jack Lenor Larsen

BELOW
3. **Hideho Tanaka** (Japanese, b. 1942)
Vanishing, 1991
Hemp fiber, stainless steel wire;
meshed, torched
11½ x 15⅛ x 15⅛ in. (29 x 38.5 x 38.5 cm)
Collection Jack Lenor Larsen

4. **Jack Lenor Larsen**
Oberon, 1969
Polyester, cotton; *devoré* printing
France
New York, Collection Cowtan & Tout

Larsen's Irish Awakening Collection, 1969, took advantage of his Irish suppliers' ability to weave luxurious wool cloths for both upholstery and drapery. *Oberon*, with its spiraling Celtic volutes, was true to the Irish theme, but it was the only textile in this collection not produced in Ireland.

Instead, Larsen looked to some of the advances the French had made in the technique of *devoré* printing, which he realized had great potential for casement fabrics. The key to this process is a ground cloth of cellulose and polyester yarns incorporated in a weave structure to create an integrated layered effect. The pattern is printed onto this cloth with an acid paste that "devours" or burns out the cellulose yarns, leaving only a polyester scrim and the denser cotton in the pattern areas. This technique gave the studio designers an affordable cloth with excellent stability and resistance to the destructive effects of light.

5. **Dale Chihuly** (American, b. 1941)
Tabak Basket Set with Black Lip Wraps, 1988
Blown glass
11 x 29 x 29 in. (27.9 x 73.7 x 73.7 cm)
East Hampton, New York,
Collection LongHouse Reserve,
Gift of Jack Lenor Larsen

FOLLOWING PAGES
6. **Jack Lenor Larsen**
Mimosa Sheer, 1990
Cotton; clipped supplementary weft patterning
Switzerland
New York, Museum of Arts & Design, Gift of Cowtan & Tout

This pattern was drawn from an antique Japanese rug of the late nineteenth century that Larsen bought for the studio's Treasure Room, an archive of potential design resources that he began in his college days. *Mimosa Sheer* illustrates the usefulness of his purchases. What makes this translucent drapery unusual is the combination of multiple wefts and jacquard patterning to create a richly varied silhouette when seen against the light.

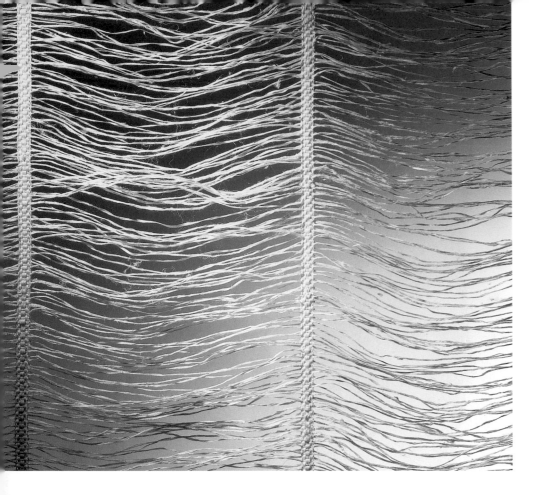

7. Jack Lenor Larsen
Bahia Blind, 2001
Linen warp, raw silk; leno construction
Thailand
New York, Collection Cowtan & Tout

Larsen originally designed this fabric in 1959 for the palaces in Oscar Niemeyer's new capital for Brazil, Brasilia. It became a hallmark of his Brasil Collection of 1959. Woven with twelve-inch (30.5 cm) weft floats between spaced warps, this cascades rhythmically in the manner of an Austrian shade. It has a dramatic silhouette and a fine shadow pattern when viewed against the light.

8. Jack Lenor Larsen
Nimbus, 1991
Saran, polyethylene monofilaments; woven, heat-shrunk
United States
New York, Collection Cowtan & Tout

In the mid-twentieth century, large windows became an important architectural element in new buildings. The Larsen design staff responded to the needs of interior designers who wished to take advantage of this contemporary innovation but without using casement fabrics that would dominate their rooms. Additional concerns were light control, interior and exterior appearance, the effects of heat and light on the fibers, and the stability of construction.

Many Larsen upholstery and drapery fabrics celebrate the inherent beauty of natural fibers, but the Design Studio never limited its work to this aesthetic. From the 1950s, Larsen explored the advantages of man-made yarns. The studio was particularly successful in developing innovative applications and adaptations of man-made fibers in casement fabrics.

Nimbus is an excellent example. Like *Cumulus* (pl. 16), this fabric was inspired by an industrial material used for insulating bomb-demolition squad suits. For both cloths, Larsen changed warp and weft diameters, altered the relationship of the synthetic yarns, and worked with temperature variations to create the casement fabrics.

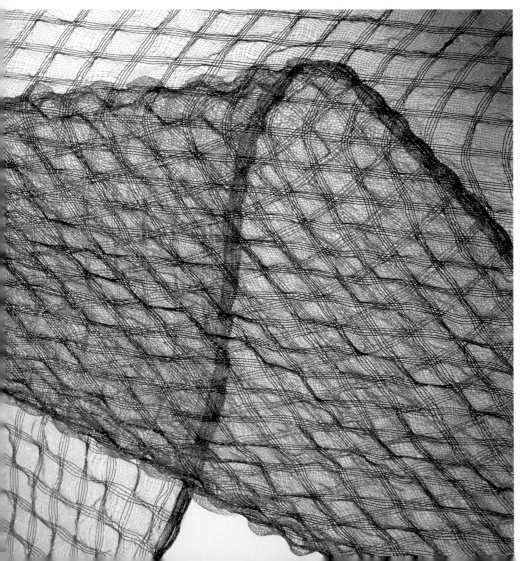

9. **Michiko Uehara**
(Japanese, b. 1949)
Scarf, c. 1995
Silk; plain weave, hand-woven
56 x 71½ in. (142.2 x 44.5 cm)
Collection Jack Lenor Larsen

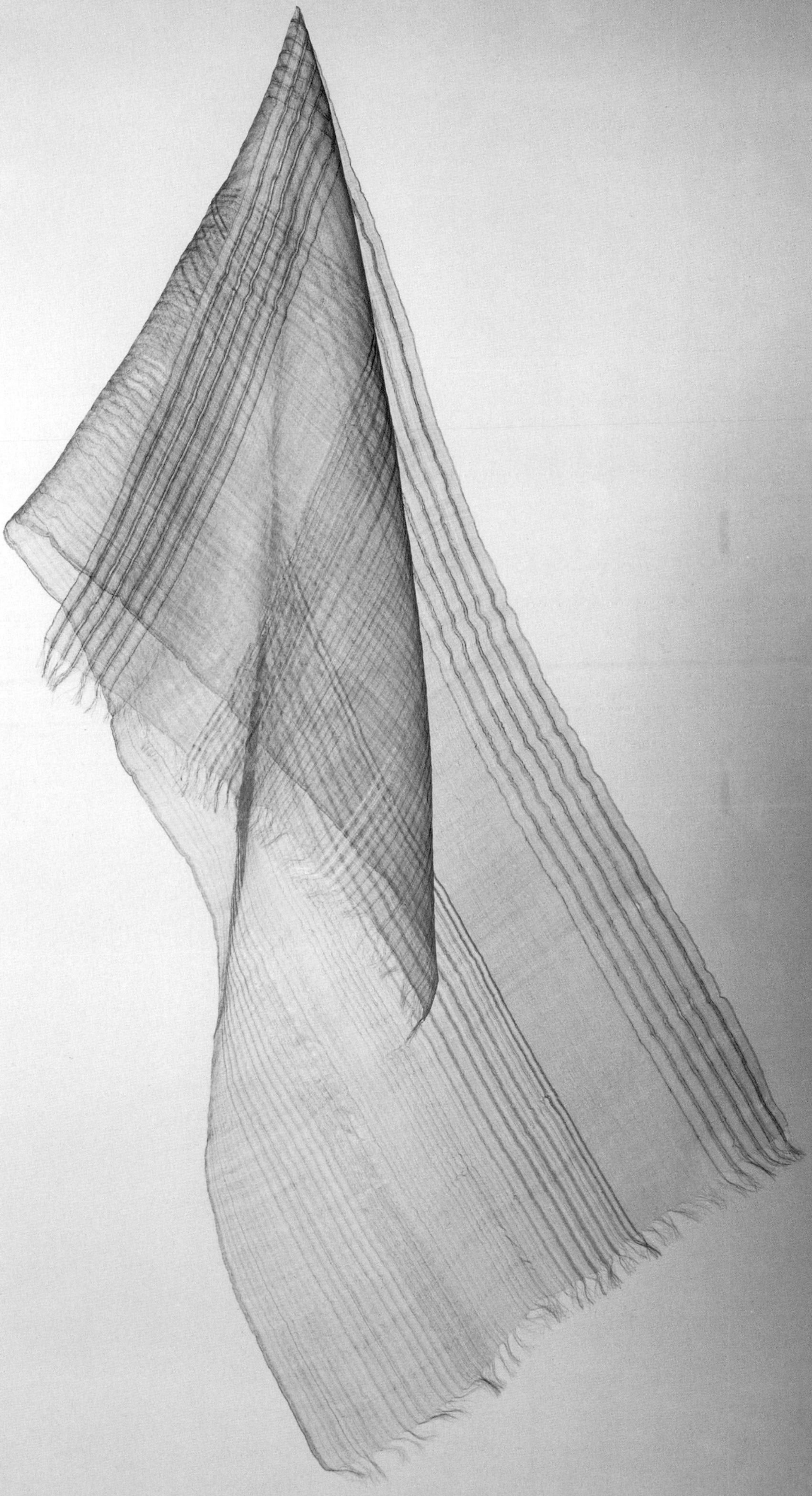

10. Jack Lenor Larsen
Onward!, 2000
Linen, silk; hand-woven
Thailand
New York, Museum of Arts & Design, Gift of Cowtan & Tout

In the late 1950s, Larsen collaborated with a small workshop in Italy to hand-weave cloth with oblique wefts as opposed to the traditional right-angle relationship of warp and weft. Utilizing the design potential of an oblique weft, *Diagonal Stripe* was added to the collection in 1959. Unfortunately, the Italian hand-weavers ceased production shortly after the fabric was introduced.

In the late 1990s Larsen was asked to create a collection inspired by some of his favorite textiles. Working with hand-weavers in Thailand, he developed a new casement fabric that showcases the fine linen warp enhanced by bold diagonals. Introduced in 2000, *Onward!* continues to be enjoyed by an appreciative clientele.

11. Jack Lenor Larsen
Eclipse, 1992
Polyester; warp-knit, powder-coated, transfer-printed, pleated
Switzerland
New York, Museum of Arts & Design, Gift of Cowtan & Tout

Classically elegant yet also practical, this solar cloth became desirable for both residences and executive offices in our omnipresent glass towers. The embellishment of the transparent metal coloring via a transfer print process did nothing to interfere with the flowing drape of the finely knit casement. A powdered aluminum backing was rolled onto the fabric, then polished to reflect light and heat, then transfer-printed to achieve the several colorations. In turning the sun's rays away from a building, it reduces air-conditioning costs. It is still available in the original three colorways, Old Gold, Bronze, and Gunmetal, which are intended to complement but not compete with both warm and cool color schemes.

12. **Jack Lenor Larsen**
Chevalier, 1978
Linen, Egyptian cotton; clipped supplementary warp patterning
Switzerland
New York, Museum of Arts & Design, Gift of Cowtan & Tout

Larsen casement fabrics are widely recognized in the industry as having an aesthetic presence that adds to an interior design scheme without overwhelming the environment. *Chevalier* amply attests to the studio's skill in balancing opaque and translucent areas in window coverings. In addition, this fabric's crêpe spun linen weft and smooth Egyptian cotton warp contribute to the effect of contrasting matte and satiny surfaces.

13. **Jack Lenor Larsen**
Hologram Leaves, 1990
Silk, linen; jacquard double-weave
Switzerland
New York, Museum of Arts & Design, Gift of Cowtan & Tout

Incorporating the unexpected into a fabric is an important goal of the Larsen team. In the late 1980s, the studio worked with a Swiss mill to explore the possibilities of sheer double cloths. Double cloth is one of Larsen's favorites (as it was for William Morris), but it has been explored most often for color patterning. In this instance, however, the interest is optical: moiré effects are created when two plain-woven fabrics are overlaid. Patterns were developed to control the size and shape of "pocketed" areas. Between 1986 and 1991 four different *Hologram* patterns were introduced into the Larsen collections.

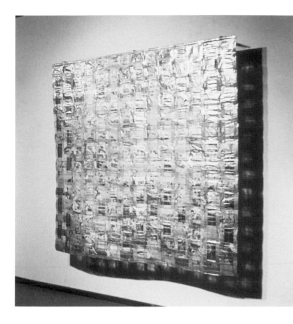

BELOW

16. **Jack Lenor Larsen**
Cumulus, 1991
Saran, polyethylene monofilaments; woven, heat-shrunk
United States
New York, Collection Cowtan & Tout

Recognizing the potential of new materials is an important aspect of the Larsen story. Two colorways of the same fabric, *Cumulus* and *Nimbus* (pl. 8), are excellent examples. Their waffle-like dimension comes from combining clear Saran monofilament yarns with a high-shrink monofilament, then immersing the woven fabric in scalding water. Popular casements that reflect a modern aesthetic, *Cumulus* and *Nimbus* also resist the damage of heat and light. They remain in production.

ABOVE

14. **Arturo A. Sandoval**
(American, b. 1942)
Gold Sky Grid, 1975
Vinyl, Mylar; veiling; machine-stitched,
interlaced, painted
60 x 60 in. (152.4 x 152.4 cm)
Collection Jack Lenor Larsen

OPPOSITE

15. **Robin Giddings** (British)
Overgarment, 1984
Machine embroidery on dissolved ground fabric
48 x 63⅜ in. (121. 9 x 186.4 cm)
New York, Museum of Arts & Design,
Gift of Jack Lenor Larsen

17. Jack Lenor Larsen

Seascape Sheer, 1977

Polyester, cotton; warp knit, *devoré* printing

France

Montreal Museum of Fine Arts, The Liliane and David M. Stewart
Collection, Gift of Jack Lenor Larsen

From the 1950s, Continental mills began producing fabrics
almost ten feet (three meters) in width. Larsen saw their
development as advantageous for window treatments. Using
the fabric's length as the width, an entire window could be
covered seamlessly with a single piece of cloth. The Larsen
Design Studio explored these possibilities, introducing a number
of new patterns employing French printers. *Seascape Sheer* is a
devoré (acid burn-out) print on a polyester and cotton casement.
Larsen had the pattern drawn to evoke the deserted beaches he
believes all urban professionals long for at 5:00 p.m.

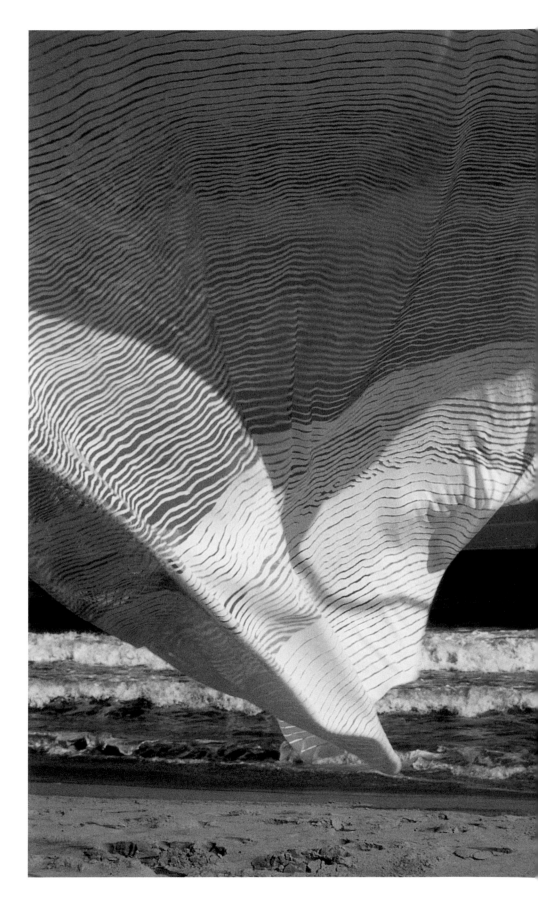

BELOW
19. **Jack Lenor Larsen**
Swan Song, 1994
Linen, silk; hand-woven, clipped supplementary weft
Thailand
New York, Museum of Arts & Design, Gift of Cowtan & Tout

Encouraging the Thai silk weavers, who have woven many Larsen textiles for thirty years, to explore the possibilities of other fibers and yarns has led to exceptional fabrics such as this. In the 1990s, the studio focused on producing casement fabrics, and it has had considerable success with its linen sheers. *Swan Song* takes advantage of the natural sheen, durability, and strength of wet spun linen warps, which also resist sunlight. Using the linen warps permitted the incorporation of silk, which is less stable when exposed to extended periods of sunlight, as a decorative, non-structural element. In addition, hand-clipped weft floats create a spontaneous, non-regimented pattern. These effects are heightened with changing interior and exterior illumination.

ABOVE
18. **Chunghi Choo** (Korean, b. 1938)
Form in Form, c. 1980
Metal mesh; folded
8 x 8 x 7¼ in. (20 x 20 x 18.5 cm)
Collection Jack Lenor Larsen

OPPOSITE
20. **Jack Lenor Larsen**
Painted Linen, 1952
Hemp, jute, rayon, paint;
hand-painted warp, woven
New York, Collection Cowtan & Tout

21. Jack Lenor Larsen
Vice Versa, 1997
Polyester; double-sided supplementary
warp pile, flame-proof
Japan
New York, Museum of Arts & Design, Gift of Cowtan & Tout

On a number of occasions Larsen immediately grasped the
potential of a fabric already developed by a manufacturer.
When a Japanese entrepreneur showed him a lightweight textile
with an unusual double-sided cut-pile surface, he realized
that, with proper coloring, it would add a new dimension to
his 1997 casement collection. *Vice Versa* was introduced in two
colorways, Oyster/Blush and Platinum/Taupe. The material is
not only reversible, but useful in controlling sound and light.
It also resists fire, sunlight, and soil.

22. Mariette Rousseau-Vermette (Canadian, b. 1926)
Hanging, 1979
Wool; twill woven, brushed
90 x 60 in. (228.6 x 152.4 cm)
Collection Jack Lenor Larsen

ABOVE

23. **Ursula Morley Price** (British, b. 1936)
White Fan #203, 1990
Stoneware; hand-built
11½ x 15 x 3 in. (29.2 x 38.1 x 7.6 cm)
East Hampton, New York, Collection
LongHouse Reserve, Purchase, Larsen Fund

LEFT

24. **Marsha D. Berentson** (American, b. 1954)
Vessel, 1984
Unglazed porcelain
8⅞ x 10 x 10 in.
(22.5 x 25.5 x 25.5 cm)
Collection Jack Lenor Larsen

OPPOSITE

25. **Marc Leuthold** (American, b. 1962)
Disk #164, 1997
Porcelain, carved
22¾ x 22¾ in. (58 x 58 cm) (without stand)
Collection Jack Lenor Larsen

TOP LEFT
26. **Unknown artist**, Japan
Futon cover, late nineteenth century
Cotton; dyed, patched
60 x 60 in. (152 x 152 cm)
Collection Jack Lenor Larsen

BOTTOM LEFT
27. **Kay Sekimachi** (American, b. 1926)
Box, 1992
Linen; double-weave, folded
8¼ x 8¼ x 8¼ in. (21 x 21 x 21 cm)
Collection Jack Lenor Larsen

OPPOSITE
28. **Jack Lenor Larsen**
Doria II, 1955
Wool; hand-spun, hand-woven
Colombia
New York, Museum of Arts & Design, Gift of Cowtan & Tout

Having discovered the design assets of hand-spun yarns in Haiti in 1952 and in Morocco soon afterward, Larsen became identified by clients for his cloths with organic surfaces of ungraded fiber, which looked as natural, inevitable, and attractive as sand or bark. European architects in the United States, particularly Marcel Breuer, first used these fabrics. Soon, leading American design firms selected them for executive offices and art collectors' homes, where their simple texture added character without competing with the art. When it was discovered that these upholsteries also retained their youthful appearance, considerably delaying the need for replacement, the *Doria* fabrics soon became the largest and most important of the hand-spuns.

In addition to the initial *Doria*, which was hand-spun and hand-woven in Colombia, several variations were developed, including *Doria Plaid* in 1966, *Doria Squares* and *Doria Stripes*, both in 1967, and *Doria Herringbone* in 1970. Several custom *Doria* fabrics were commissioned for Air Force One in 1969. A new *Doria* Collection was introduced in 2003.

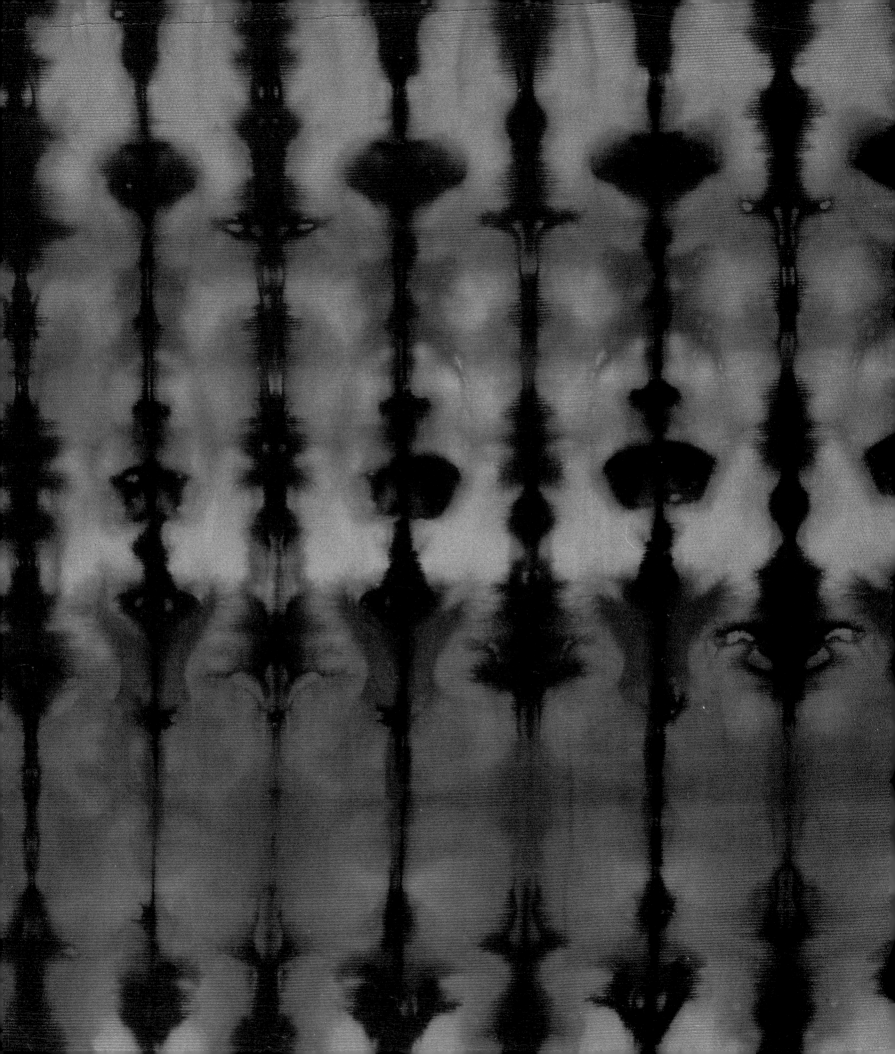

29. **Jack Lenor Larsen / Eliza Wilcox** (British)
Chan Chan, 1964
Cotton; fold-dyed
Kenya
East Hampton, New York, Collection LongHouse Reserve

The Larsen design team's diverse range of fabrics derives from international connections and willingness to coordinate a variety of production needs. Chan Chan's rep-weave ground cloth was woven in Switzerland, then shipped to Kenya where 50-yard (45-meter) lengths were patterned with the traditional West African fold-dyeing techniques. To maintain consistency in the pattern, fifty Kenyan women, standing in a long line, first pleated the long bolt of cloth, then repeatedly tied it to make the pattern—all to a drumbeat.

Here, the manipulated cloth clearly expresses the pattern of dye absorption: pattern and process are totally integrated. A similar pattern, created with a cotton velvet ground cloth was called *Chimu*. Both fabrics had to be discontinued in 1967 after Eliza Wilcox, who developed the design process for the fabric and supervised its production, was killed in a car accident.

30. **Olga de Amaral** (Colombian, b. 1932)
Tierra y Oro #5, 1985
Horsehair, wool, gold leaf;
plain weave
34¼ x 48½ in. (87 x 123.2 cm)
East Hampton, New York,
Collection LongHouse Reserve,
Gift of Mr. and Mrs. Stanley Marcus

34. Don Wight (American, b. 1925)
for Larsen Studio
Leaves of Grass, 1971
Cotton velvet; batik
United States
East Hampton, New York, Collection LongHouse Reserve

In the early 1950s many Larsen textiles were custom orders, often hand-woven in the studio. Others were woven at Larsen's New Jersey mill. By the mid-1950s, however, the volume of orders changed this situation: the Design Studio expanded to create patterns and to choose color palettes for production offshore. Since then designs have been realized among a widening variety of production sources, from high-tech industrial mills to hand production in the Third World.

One exception to this out-sourcing was Larsen's development of batik velvets produced inside the company in the 1960s and 1970s. Under the supervision of Win Anderson, then president of Larsen Design Studio, a system was devised to print hot wax-resist patterns, with repeats of up to 36 x 50 inches (91 x 127 cm). After the wax had set, the prepared fabric, usually 50-yard (45-meter) lengths, left the studio to be dyed, dewaxed, and often dyed again. The studio produced these batik velvets until the early 1980s. Wooden blocks for the *Leaves of Grass* pattern were drawn for the Larsen Studio by the American designer Don Wight.

35. Unknown artist, Japan
Bone container, *c.* 300 CE
Unglazed ceramic; coiled
13⅜ x 17 x 10⅜ in.
(33.9 x 43.2 x 26.4 cm)
East Hampton, New York,
Collection LongHouse Reserve

36. **Unknown artist**, Colombia
Fish scalers, *c.* 1000 CE
Flint embedded in clay with incised patterns
10½ x 3¼ x 1⅛ in. (26.6 x 9.5 x 3 cm)
East Hampton, New York,
Collection LongHouse Reserve,
Gift of Jack Lenor Larsen

PREVIOUS PAGES
37. Jack Lenor Larsen
Bas Relief, 1969
Cotton; resist, resin and block-printed
Switzerland
East Hampton, New York, Collection LongHouse Reserve

Larsen believes that design is more than just pattern: it is the
creative integration of many elements—including use over
time—to produce an overall effect. The most remarkable
characteristic of the Larsen Studio was its aesthetic as well as
its practical knowledge. The rather archaic look of this textile is
reinforced by the techniques employed to make it. Inspiration
came from processes then available at the oldest textile printing
plant in Europe (said to date from the thirteenth century), and
also from Assyrian reliefs at the British Museum.

Starting with fine cotton velvet woven and finished for Larsen
in Italy, the Swiss printer applied a resist pattern in pine pitch
before immersing the cloth in earthen pits filled with natural
indigo dye. After days of cold-water washing, the blue-and-
white pattern was hand-printed with large blocks wrapped in
felt. Then the fabric was sent to the United States, where a
silicone finish and acrylic latex backing were applied. *Bas Relief*
was introduced in 1969 as part of the Reflection, Forms and
Nature Collection.

TOP RIGHT

38. Peter Voulkos (American, 1924–2002)
Vessel, 1959–60
Hand-built stoneware
39½ x 19 x 10½ in. (100.5 x 48.3 x 26.7 cm)
New York, Museum of Arts & Design,
Gift of Jack Lenor Larsen

BOTTOM RIGHT

39. Unknown artist, N'dbele people, South Africa
Apron, early twentieth century
Beading over cotton canvas
13¾ x 17⅝ in. (35 x 45 cm)
Collection Jack Lenor Larsen

40. **Lenore Tawney** (American, b. 1907)
Boxed Collage, 1962
Antique book pages, watercolor
9 x 10 x 2⅜ in. (22.9 x 25.4 x 6 cm)
Collection Jack Lenor Larsen

41. **Jack Lenor Larsen**
Solarus, 1985
Worsted, cotton; warp-faced leno
Scotland
New York, Collection Cowtan & Tout

Warp-faced leno weave is a rare fabric structure invented by
a prisoner during World War II, who bent pipe cleaners into
a three-dimensional diagram, allowing him to experiment with
a variety of interlacings. The structure requires the horizontal
placement of major warp elements, creating tapestry-like
pattern capability in a very durable cloth. The Larsen design
team worked with Scottish weavers to develop several of these
distinctive upholstery fabrics. The bold patterns and ribbed
texture gave them a natural appeal, with an extreme durability
and a resistance to soiling that are now legendary.

42. **Bradley Miller** (American, b. 1950)
Porcelain Sphere #2, 1996
Tumbled porcelain, nylon
6 x 6 x 6 in. (15.2 x 15.2 x 15.2 cm)
Collection Jack Lenor Larsen

43. **Mary Caroline Richards** (American, 1916–1999)
Box, 1992
Painted stoneware; slab built, painted
8 x 8 x 8 in. (20.3 x 20.3 x 20.3 cm)
Collection Jack Lenor Larsen

44. **Unknown artist**, Native American Tribe, United States
Beaded skirt, late nineteenth century
26½ x 17¾ in. (67.3 x 45.1 cm)
Collection Jack Lenor Larsen

45. **Jack Lenor Larsen**
Luxor, 1980
Wool; twill weave
Uruguay
East Hampton, New York, Collection LongHouse Reserve

In addition to dramatic signature pieces, the Larsen Studio designs numerous upholstery and casement fabrics of quiet but distinctive quality. Color is always an important factor, and much care is taken to simulate colors in nature through the juxtaposition of yarns of varying hues. Hand-spun yarns of an extremely silky wool were hand-woven for *Luxor* in colorways including Woodhue, Sugar Plum, Blue Spruce, and Night Violet. The name *Luxor* was intended to underline the aura of luxury created by its fine wool and nuanced hues.

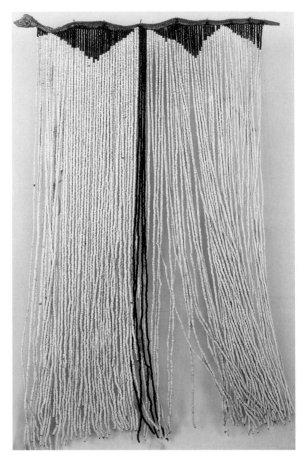

46. **Jack Lenor Larsen**
Horsecloth, 1954
Linen, cotton, goat hair, mohair, wool; woven fabric
United States
Montreal Museum of Fine Arts, The Liliane and David M. Stewart Collection, Gift of Jack Lenor Larsen

Throughout the 1950s, textiles such as *Horsecloth*, with its natural fibers and hand-woven look, were the hallmark fabrics of the company. Larsen's understanding of the texture, feel, and subtle, spontaneous character of hand-woven cloth allowed him to retain these qualities with power looms, even in circumstances that greatly speeded up production. Working with the Bolan Mill in New Jersey, the company devised many labor- and cost-saving systems that enabled them to maintain a diverse but low-volume inventory—an important consideration for a young company with minimal capital.

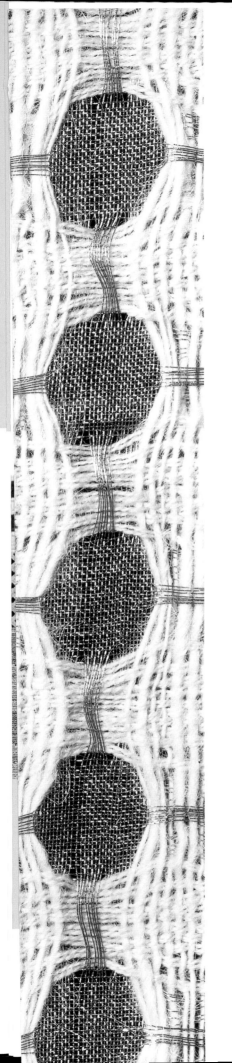

47. Jack Lenor Larsen
Waterford, 1969
Wool, mohair, Lurex metallic gimp; woven fabric
Ireland
Montreal Museum of Fine Arts, The Liliane and David M. Stewart
Collection, Gift of Jack Lenor Larsen

Larsen's vision, knowledge of historical textiles, and extensive
technical background engender tremendous respect within the
textile industry and have allowed him to form special relationships with mills around the world. Sam Schepps and, later, John
Orr, the owners of an Irish weaving mill, worked with the Design
Studio on a number of projects for more than twenty years and
often ended up using equipment and materials in innovative
ways in order to achieve the vitality of Larsen's concept.

On several occasions Larsen exploited the dramatic, reflective
quality of metal yarn to advantage in designs for casement
fabrics. For *Waterford* he combined silky wools and a fine
metal gimp in a traditional honeycomb-weave structure to
create a surface that is transparent by day, but opaque and
light-reflecting by night.

48. Chunghi Choo (Korean, b. 1938)
Two Decanters, 1980
Copper, silver plate; electro-formed
Each 5¼ x 5 x 5¼ in. (13.3 x 12.7 x 13.3 cm)
New York, Museum of Arts & Design,
Gift of Jack Lenor Larsen

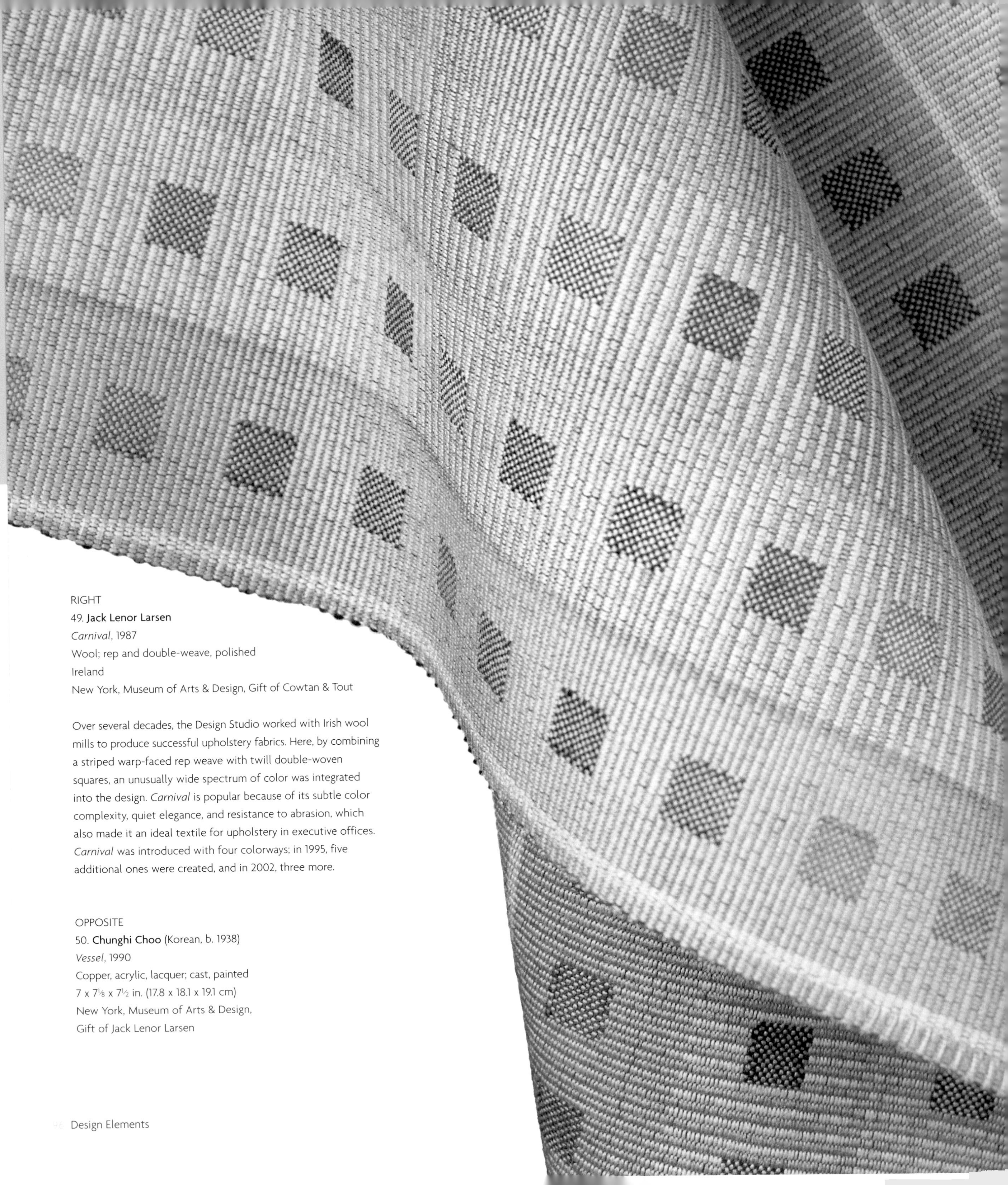

RIGHT

49. Jack Lenor Larsen
Carnival, 1987
Wool; rep and double-weave, polished
Ireland
New York, Museum of Arts & Design, Gift of Cowtan & Tout

Over several decades, the Design Studio worked with Irish wool
mills to produce successful upholstery fabrics. Here, by combining
a striped warp-faced rep weave with twill double-woven
squares, an unusually wide spectrum of color was integrated
into the design. *Carnival* is popular because of its subtle color
complexity, quiet elegance, and resistance to abrasion, which
also made it an ideal textile for upholstery in executive offices.
Carnival was introduced with four colorways; in 1995, five
additional ones were created, and in 2002, three more.

OPPOSITE

50. Chunghi Choo (Korean, b. 1938)
Vessel, 1990
Copper, acrylic, lacquer; cast, painted
7 x 7⅛ x 7½ in. (17.8 x 18.1 x 19.1 cm)
New York, Museum of Arts & Design,
Gift of Jack Lenor Larsen

51. Jack Lenor Larsen
Hills of Home, 1975
Silk; hand screen-printed
United States
East Hampton, New York, Collection LongHouse Reserve

When Larsen introduced *Hills of Home* in the early 1970s as part of the Great Colors of China Collection, this large, dramatic pattern evoking an idyllic landscape made a bold statement. The intention was to simulate a pleasurable experience in the country rather than to represent a particular time and place.

52. Jack Lenor Larsen
Primavera, 1959
Cotton velvet; hand screen-printed
United States
East Hampton, New York, Collection LongHouse Reserve

Primavera, inspired by Gustav Klimt's paintings, was the most successful printed velvet in the industry to that date. Previous attempts at printing on velvet had been obstructed by the long, thick pile of the fabric. After much experiment, Larsen was able to weave a pile low enough for full dye penetration, with no loss of color intensity. This complex print uses seven screens and takes advantage of overprinting techniques to produce both subtle and dramatic effects of hue. The fabric was available in ten colorways, and its durability as well as beauty soon made it especially popular for upholstery.

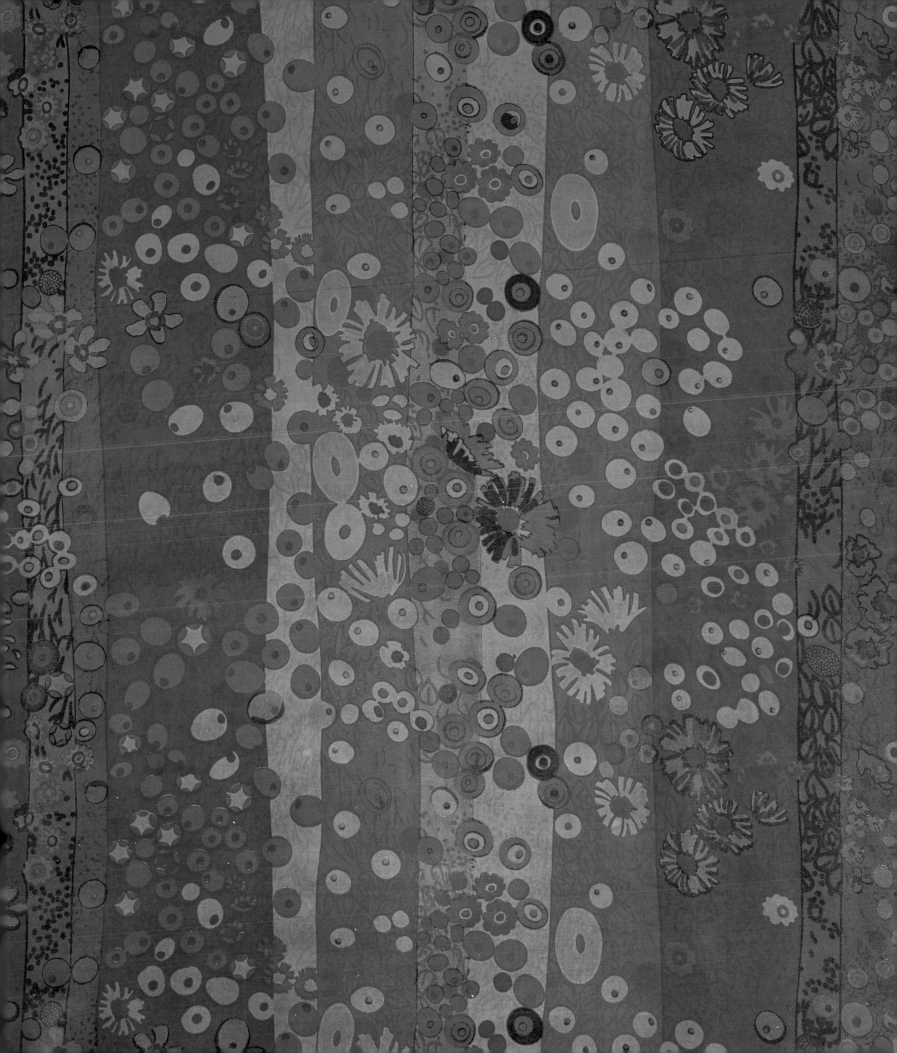

OPPOSITE
53. **Unknown artist**, Indonesia
Skirt cloth, early twentieth century
Cotton, gold leaf; batik
68½ x 39⅛ in. (174 x 99.5 cm)
Collection Jack Lenor Larsen

LEFT
54. **Jack Lenor Larsen**
Spice Garden, 1954
Linen; hand screen-printed
United States
East Hampton, New York, Collection LongHouse Reserve

Spice Garden, the company's first printed upholstery fabric, fulfilled a leading aesthetic of the 1950s. The unusual use of color with a pattern of randomly scattered flowers was unified by subtle printed texture overlays. A popular pattern for thirty years, *Spice Garden* was printed on a number of different ground fabrics, including linen, cotton, cotton and silk, and velvet.

Initially drawn and hand-printed by June Groff in her studio, the design soon inspired such demand that production was moved to commercial printers in New England and Germany. At least ten colorways were developed, each requiring up to nine screens.

FOLLOWING PAGES
55. **Jack Lenor Larsen**
Happiness, 1967
Rayon, cotton, mohair; hand screen-printed
United States and West Germany
New York, Collection Cowtan & Tout

Certain Larsen designs have captured the public's imagination and are recognized as hallmarks of the studio. *Happiness* remained in production for almost twenty years as a drapery and upholstery fabric and has also been used since 1975 as a jacquard rug pattern. Production of this fabric was complex because some of the same pattern areas were printed with three different colors.

According to company records, the design was inspired by a Chinese robe and Ming Dynasty embroideries in the collection of the Seattle Art Museum. It was introduced with four colorways—Amethyst Quartz, Ming Gold, Lacquer Red, and Mandarin Blue—as part of the 1968 Kublai Khan Collection. By 1977, three additional colorways were produced, Red Earth, Roselake, and Blonde.

56. **Unknown artist**, Northwest India
Blouse, early twentieth century
Silk on cotton, mirrors; modified chain stitch, French knots
27⅝ x 28⅜ in. (70 x 72 cm)
Collection Jack Lenor Larsen

57. **Jack Lenor Larsen**
Conquistador, 1966
Cotton velvet; batik
United States
East Hampton, New York, Collection LongHouse Reserve

Conquistador, introduced as part of the 1967 Andean Collection, was particularly successful and soon became one of the signature cloths of the company. In a note in the company archive, Larsen writes that "*Conquistador* is my concept of how an Inca might handle a baroque motif, that is, flatly and without the robust movement typical in Europe. More like the stone walls of Peru." The cloth was dyed twice for a contrapuntal vibration of hues close in value, such as bronze and amethyst, or amber and brown to suggest tortoiseshell. Though the printing technique is the same as that used for *Leaves of Grass*, here the Spanish colonial motif is scaled to fit upholstery cushioning, and the look is one of great antiquity.

58. Jack Lenor Larsen
Turkoman, 1978
Worsted, cotton; warp-faced leno
Scotland
East Hampton, New York, Collection LongHouse Reserve

Larsen is celebrated in the industry for his ability to see the
aesthetic potential of textile technology. In the mid-1970s on
a trip to England, he noticed some chairs with a rather
undistinguished faux needlepoint upholstery. Noting the unusual
tapestry-like surface, he realized it might capture the essence of
some types of Middle Eastern and Central Asian tapestry-woven
rugs. When *Turkoman* was introduced as part of the studio's
Premises Collection, there were a number of different colorways,
from the traditional deep reds and blues of kilims to the then-
fashionable pale hues of dhurries. This textile has since received
considerable attention for its ironclad durability..

59. Priscilla Henderson (American, b. 1942)
Basket, c. 1980
Rattan, wood; woven, incised, painted, lacquered
14 x 20½ x 20½ in. (35.6 x 52.1 x 52.1 cm)
Collection Jack Lenor Larsen

60. **Unknown artist**, Kuba people, Zaïre
Skirt cloth, early twentieth century
Raffia palm-fiber, embroidered patchwork, pom-pom fringe
30 x 365 in. (76.2 x 912 cm)
Collection Jack Lenor Larsen

61. **Unknown artist**, Nez Perce tribe, United States
Bag, early twentieth century
Corn husks twined with tapestry joins
24 x 16½ in. (61 x 42 cm)
Collection Jack Lenor Larsen

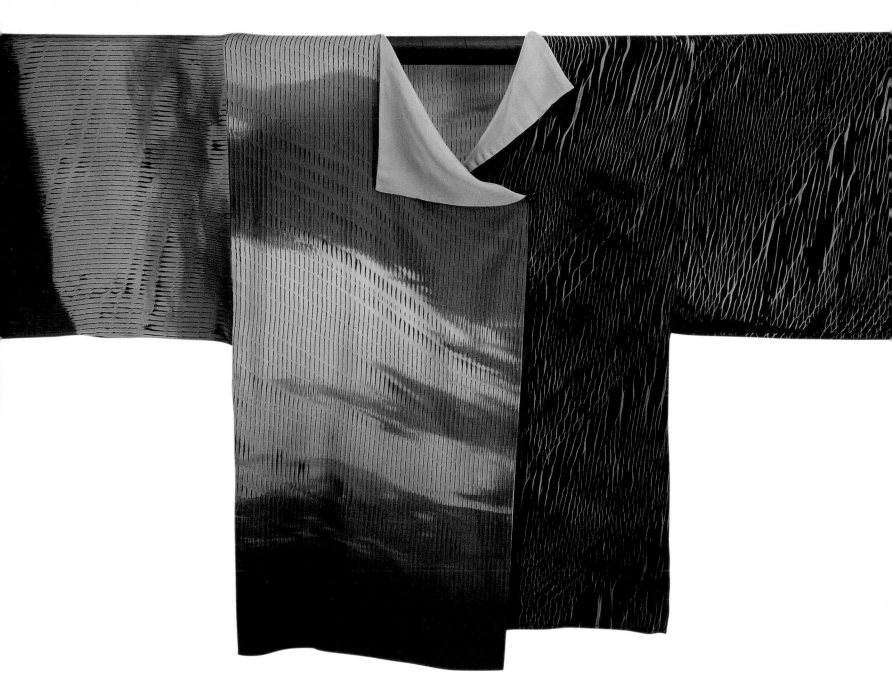

62. **Ana Lisa Hedstrom** (American, b. 1943)
Silk Blouse, 1982
Silk; fold-dyed, sewn
30 x 45 in. (76.2 x 114.3 cm)
New York, Museum of Arts & Design,
Gift of Jack Lenor Larsen

63. **Warren Seelig** (American, b. 1946)
Cincture #2, 1979
Cotton; double cloth
66½ x 18 in. (169 x 45.5 cm)
Collection Jack Lenor Larsen

64. Jack Lenor Larsen
Magnum, 1970
Cotton, Mylar, vinyl, nylon, polyester; machine-embroidered
United States
East Hampton, New York, Collection LongHouse Reserve

Perhaps the most famous of all Larsen fabrics, *Magnum* was initially developed for the act curtain of Symphony Hall in the Phoenix Civic Plaza, Arizona, a commission requiring 600 yards (550 meters) of material. The studio was asked to simulate the hand-embroidered mirror-work fabrics of India, but in the colors of the Southwest's Kachina dolls. The Larsen designers experimented extensively to find the ideal materials and technical adjustments of mechanical embroidery equipment. The embroidery pattern chosen so completely covers the Mylar ground that only small square "mirrors" remain. When introduced into the Larsen collections in 1973, *Magnum* was available in the curtain's Flame colorway, as well as Golden Topaz and several other choices. A second theater curtain commission, by Skidmore, Owings & Merrill, resulted in the colorway shown here. The design was not discontinued until 1992. The Phoenix curtain, installed in 1972, is still in use, delighting audiences with its changing reflections as they wait for performances to begin.

65. Unknown artist, Japan
Kimono, c. 1930
Silk; warp ikat
59 x 49 in. (149 x 124 cm)
Collection Jack Lenor Larsen

66. Jack Lenor Larsen
Remoulade, 1956
Cotton, wool, Lurex, jute, silk, rayon; woven fabric
United States
East Hampton, New York, Collection LongHouse Reserve

Remoulade, the French sauce of various spicy ingredients, is the name Larsen gave this heavy cloth with dozens of different yarns in random repeat. It became the star of his Spice Garden Collection and one of the fabrics that made him famous in the 1950s. Initially these cloths were hand-woven, but when demand exceeded the studio's production capabilities, a solution had to be found. Working with an Italian weaver with a small mill in New Jersey, Larsen was able to replicate these textiles with power looms. Although the looms, with three warp beams and dangling spools, could only weave fifteen yards (fourteen meters) a day, they did so, dependably.

67. Jack Lenor Larsen
Laotian Ikat, 1972
Silk, metallic gimp: hand-woven, weft ikat
Thailand
New York, Museum of Arts & Design, Gift of Jack Lenor Larsen

Since the 1950s, Larsen has worked with numerous traditional weavers, including workshops in Haiti, Mexico, and Morocco, adapting their skills to produce contemporary fabrics for the interiors market. With Thai Silk, a company founded shortly after World War II by the legendary Jim Thompson, Larsen developed a number of distinctive fabrics. Among the most dramatic were the ikat cloths. Originally the technique had been used to create short lengths of fabric for wrapped skirts, but Larsen persuaded the weavers to create a heavier-weight cloth in continuous lengths for an upholstery fabric.

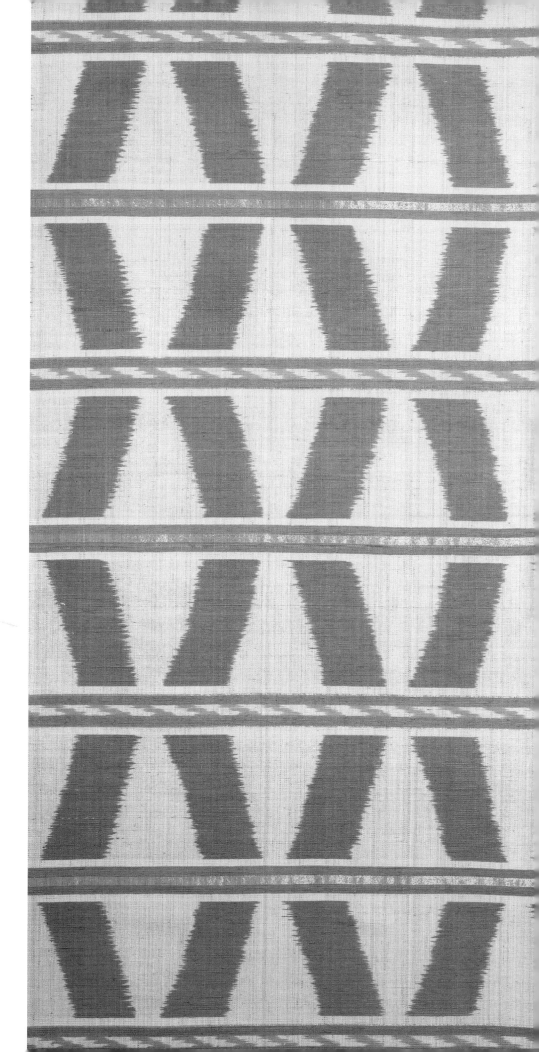

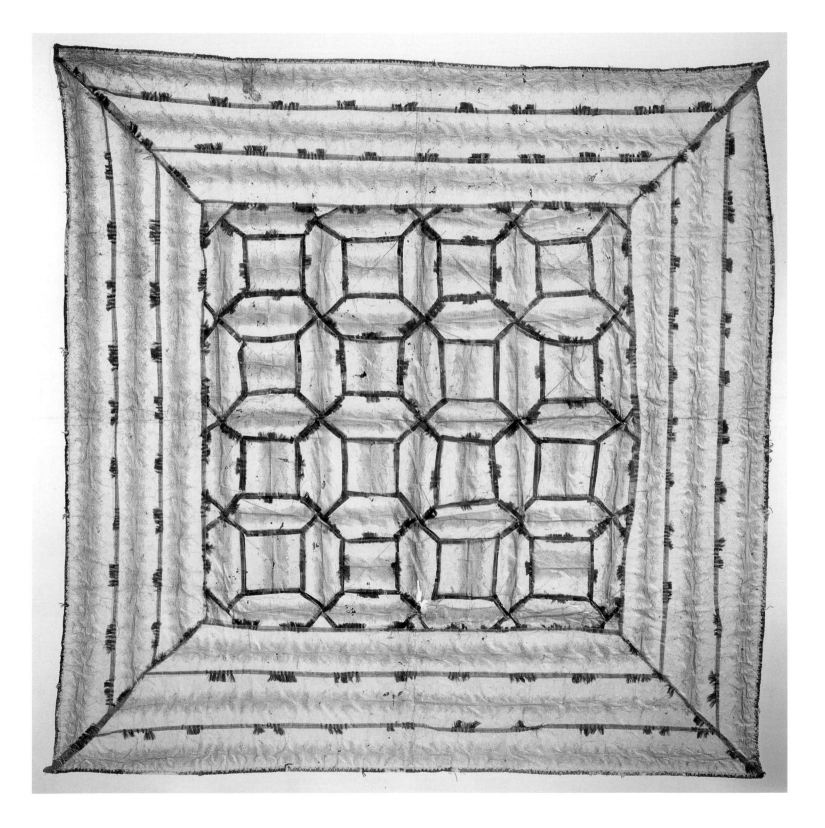

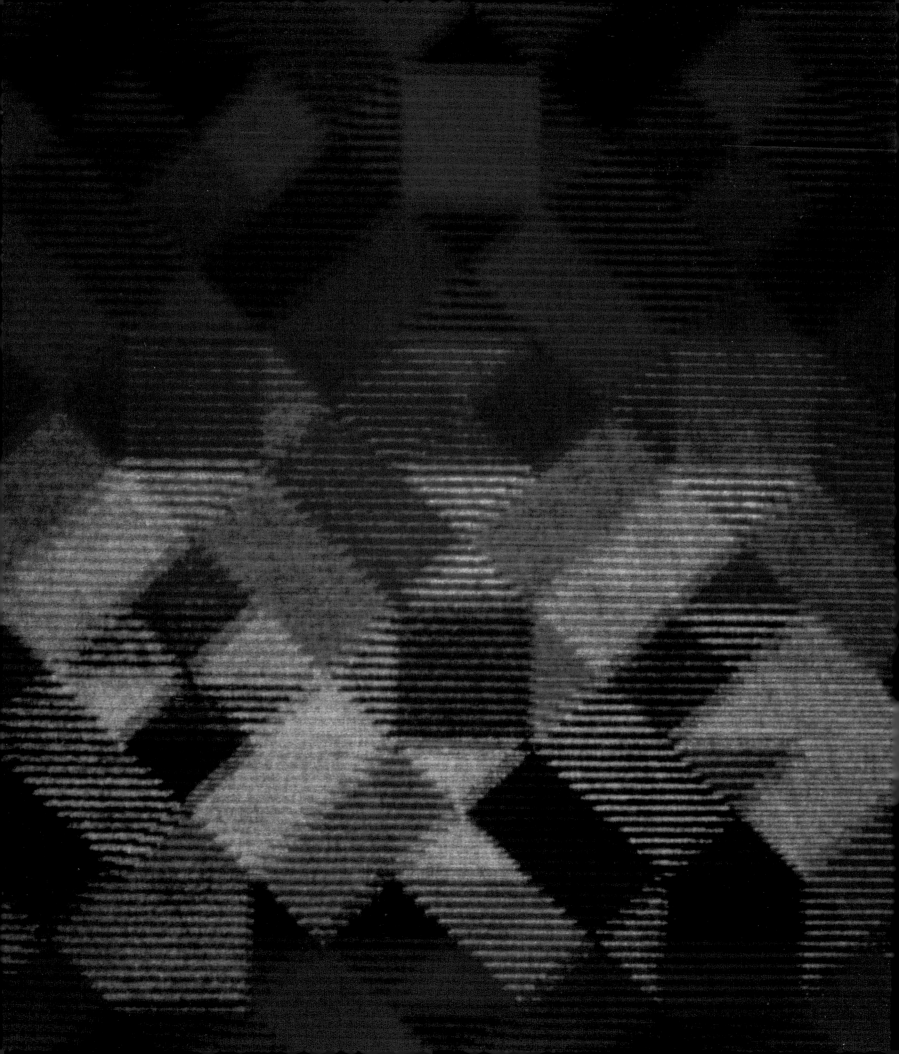

72. Jack Lenor Larsen
Labyrinth, 1981
Worsted, cotton; warp-faced leno
Scotland
New York, Collection Cowtan & Tout

This fabric is unique, since only the Larsen design team has the aesthetic sensitivity and technical know-how to create such complexity of color. The majority of textile designers who work with woven structures are trained to develop pattern through weft manipulation. Warp-faced weaves, such as this unusual variation of a leno structure, and the better-known "jacquard tapestry" structure, present a particular challenge. The few mills that produce these heavier upholstery fabrics usually choose more traditional color palettes, with the result that fabrics with these weave constructions are often ignored by discriminating interior designers. For many years, Larsen designs were among the very few exceptions to this rule. Like other such Larsen textiles with rich and distinctive color palettes, *Labyrinth* is a *tour de force* in its sumptuous hues and warp-faced weave. It is much admired within the profession.

73. Guy Houdouin (French, b. 1940)
Etoile de Patak II, 1987
Polychrome paper sheets; hand-dyed, interlaced
31 x 31 in. (78.7 x 78.7 cm)
Collection Jack Lenor Larsen

Form and Structure

Jack Lenor Larsen, *Architecture*
(detail of pl. 102)

Larsen's respect for form and structure is the logical outgrowth of his background in architecture: "I wasn't taught fabric design. I was taught architectural design. Through weaving I made a transition from architecture to fabric." In such fabric designs as *Academia*, 1973 (pl. 82), he sought an architectural purity of form, proportion, and structure. Metallic gimp adds a lively glow while the restrained palette emphasizes the cloth's subtle geometry. The same delight in construction is evident in Larsen's casement of machine-made bobbin lace called *Crystal Palace*, 1964 (pl. 74). Bold patterning based on the structure of the fabric is reflected in his *Triad*, 1993 (pl. 89), which gains further interest through the use of complex stitching over the basic pattern.[1] The timeless, even archetypal geometries of triangles are celebrated in this cloth. Form and structure are revealed by the fabrication techniques Larsen selects, making his fabrics sympathetic to the pared-down simplicity of modern corporate and domestic interiors. Richard Landis, a brilliant and obsessive weaver inspired by the natural world around him,

often used hundreds of different hues of yarn to create his memorable essays in the gradation of color, as in *Hanging* (pl. 95). Larsen deeply admired both the artist and his work, and paid homage to him in the fabric he called *Landis II*, 1982 (pl. 96). Displayed in complex geometry, its vibrating colors appear to shift constantly, as light does over a landscape vista, while following the disciplined structure of the weave.

In building his art collections, Larsen has focused primarily on abstract forms that suggest, rather than literally depict, the world of nature, or geometric forms that reveal the interplay of materials, structure, and technique. However, a small number of works in the Larsen collections represent the human form, such as the entwined bodies that cover the swelling surfaces of ceramicist Rudy Autio's *Drum Lummond Ladies and Lippizano, c.* 1983 (pl. 92). An imposing African carved wood throne made for Dahomey royalty is supported on four caryatids that lift the sitter symbolically above the earth (pl. 78). The rough-hewn power of such forms, expressed through the animal world, is captured by the American studio furniture artist Judy Kensley McKie, whose bronze *Lion Bench*, 1994 (pl. 105), commands attention and respect.

Larsen's taste is generally inclined to more abstract references to the body, as seen in the works of ceramicist Richard Devore (pls. 93, 99). Devore's sensuous sculptural vessels explore and celebrate the curves, recesses, and orifices of the body. Consistent with Larsen's dedication to the abstract rather than the literal are many works that allude to the body metaphorically. Subtle gradations of color cover the surfaces of vessels by the noted American ceramicist Toshiko Takaezu, as seen in *Closed Form, c.* 1992 (pl. 87). Even when modest in physical size, these forms convey a majesty and monumentality uniquely identified with this artist. Made of bent wood, Linda Bills's *Japanese Armor*, 1985 (pl. 91), implies a body by its absence, in a haunting echo of the human form. Stephen Proctor's *Folding Table, c.* 1965 (pl. 80), is carved to suggest the muscular form of a dancer. The tabletop is also articulated to tilt upward, much like a human joint.

In many of the objects that Larsen has acquired, form, structure, and materials hark back to nature as the ultimate source of design. By basket-maker/ sculptor Dorothy Gill Barnes, *Corkscrew Willow Cube*, 1999 (pl. 85), is made of pale willow branches entwined to create a box-like form; it bridges the worlds of the organic and the geometric. For Larsen, art objects like this connect with his love of gardening and nature. Attenuated and eccentric floral forms are suggested by the metalsmith Chunghi Choo in *Lily Vase*, 1980 (pl. 98). Their animated organic shapes are reminiscent of both exotic flowers and the swirling draperies of the *fin-de-siècle* dancer Loïe Fuller captured in a stop-action image.

The flowing lines of Art Nouveau design are forecast in an imposing Japanese stoneware vessel, 1500–1400 BCE (pl. 100). The profile of the vessel is stretched heavenward, while the intertwining tendrils forming the lip suggest the tumescent growth of plants in the springtime, or the visually striking patterns created when waves of water collide. The ceramic forms of Dame Lucie Rie (pl. 81) and Hans

Coper (pl. 90), the two leading figures in British ceramics in the second half of the twentieth century, are studies in proportion. Both are intimately linked to the perceived form, proportion, and structure of the human body. Refinement of surface, graceful forms, and beautiful colors combine to give special appeal to the work of Australian ceramicist Gwyn Hansen Piggott. The artist's *Echo #4*, 1999 (pl. 84), is a cluster of six delicately shaded vessels made with a glassy Limoges porcelain body. These simple forms have been glazed and wood-fired to create an ensemble of shapes that conveys the mirror surface of still water, the palette of soft colors seen only at dawn, and the chill of winter ice.

Wharton Esherick was an acknowledged dean of American art furniture in the twentieth century. Gifted as both a sculptor and a furniture maker, Esherick echoed the muscularity and bone structure of the human body in his expressionistic forms. Larsen considers him among "the greatest furniture designers of all time, whose works speak an international language of beauty, strength, and refinement."

The Larsen collections contain a table and chairs in hickory wood by Esherick, dated to 1939 (pl. 79), which exemplify the simplicity of the designer's style at the end of his life. Contrasting with these works in natural wood is a unique bench, *c*. 1950 (pl. 76), made of pine and painted a brilliant strawberry red. The gentle curve of the bench seat is supported at one point by a series of caterpillar-like legs, with an open extension that creates a sense of movement while maintaining the powerful simplicity of the bench's form.

Technical virtuosity can also produce extraordinary patterning, as illustrated by a group of baskets from the Philippines (pl. 104). The complexity of their construction, of thin strips of bamboo woven in complex patterns, is belied by the simplicity of their sculptural shapes. They typify the objects in the Larsen collections that were selected for the ways in which their purposes are illuminated by their forms, substances, and techniques of fabrication. Lightweight yet strong, they represent a perfect union of form, material, and function.

D.R.McF.

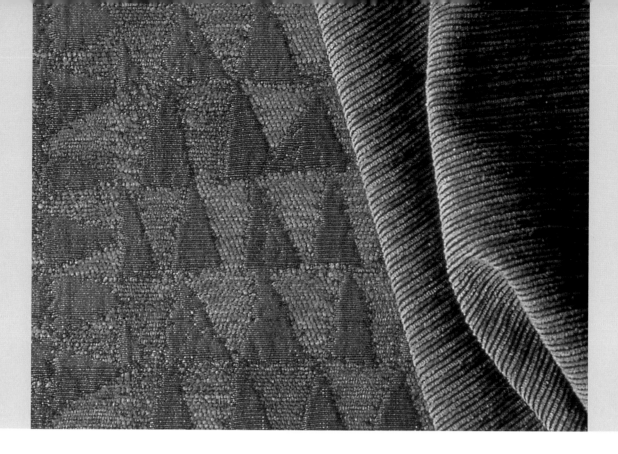

[1] Krista Stack Pawar, "Larsen: Inside the Company," in *Interplay: Perspectives on the Design Legacy of Jack Lenor Larsen*, ed. Denise Guerin and Stephanie Watson, Minneapolis MN (Goldstein Museum of Design/University of Minnesota) 2001.

Jack Lenor Larsen, *Triad* (detail of pl. 89) shown alongside *Royal Velvet*, 1993

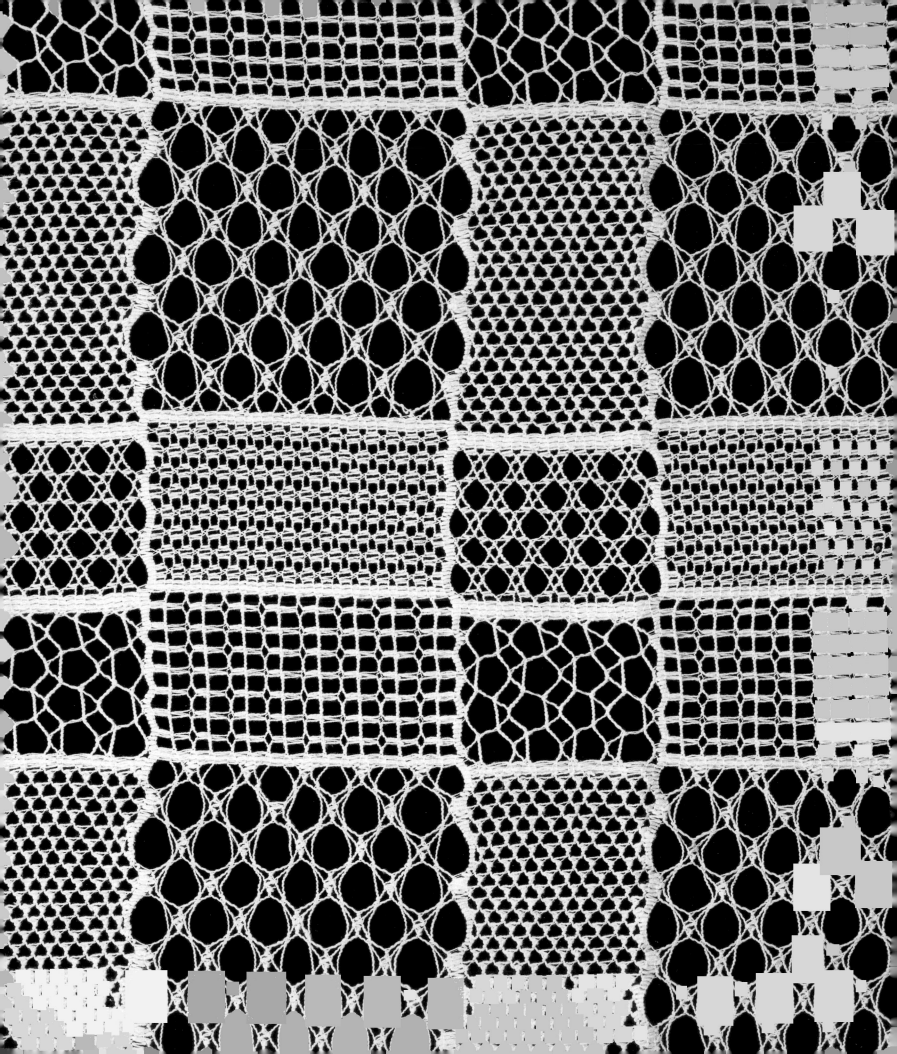

OPPOSITE
74. Jack Lenor Larsen
Crystal Palace, 1964
Cotton; Nottingham lace
Germany
Montreal Museum of Fine Arts, The Liliane and David M. Stewart
Collection, Gift of Jack Lenor Larsen

With the growing popularity of lace in the nineteenth century,
the textile industry turned its attention to the challenge of
mechanizing a hand process that was traditionally very labor-
intensive and expensive. By 1850 machines had been developed
that could efficiently simulate a variety of the ground structures
used to create bobbin lace.

Crystal Palace was inspired by the sample blankets that mills
produce for designers to test color and weave possibilities.
Using the grid layout of the sample blanket and adapting its
function of displaying many similar patterns on a single cloth,
Larsen created a lace casement that remained in the company's
showrooms for seven years. It was wide enough to permit
seamless window walls; the vertical bands insure stability.

LEFT
75. Alev Ebüzziya Siesbye (Turkish, b. 1938)
Vase, 2001
Stoneware; coiled, glazed
16 x 10 x 10 in. (40.6 x 25.3 x 25.3 cm)
East Hampton, New York, Collection LongHouse Reserve,
Purchase, Katzenberg Fund

BELOW
76. Wharton Esherick (American, 1887–1970)
Bench, c. 1950
Painted pine
16¾ x 85⅝ x 31 in. (42.5 x 217.5 x 78.8 cm)
East Hampton, New York, Collection LongHouse Reserve,
Purchase, Larsen Fund

LEFT
77. **Wharton Esherick** (American, 1887–1970)
Archway for Curtis Bok house, from passageway
between dining room and foyer, Radnor,
Pennsylvania, c. 1933
Carved chestnut
102 x 91 x 17 in. (259.1 x 231.1 x 43.2 cm)
Collection Jack Lenor Larsen

BELOW
78. **Unknown artist**, Dahomey (Republic of Benin)
Throne, late nineteenth century
Hardwood monolith; carved
32 x 20¾ x 13 in. (81.3 x 52.7x 33 cm)
East Hampton, New York, Collection LongHouse Reserve,
Gift of Jack Lenor Larsen

ABOVE
79. **Wharton Esherick** (American, 1887–1970)
Dining table, 1939
Hickory, phenol
26½ x 62½ x 40½ in. (67.3 x 158.8 x 102.9 cm)
Collection Jack Lenor Larsen

Chairs, 1939
Hickory, rawhide
32 x 16½ x 15½ in. (81.3 x 41.9 x 39.4 cm) each
Collection Jack Lenor Larsen

80. **Stephen Proctor** (British, b. 1948)
Folding Table, c. 1965
Carved and ebonized wood
28½ x 23 in. (72.4 x 58.4 cm)
Collection Jack Lenor Larsen

81. **Dame Lucie Rie** (British, b. Austria, 1902–1995)
Tall Form, 1976
Thrown porcelain, *sgraffito*
9¼ x 5¼ x 5¼ in. (23.7 x 13.1 x 13.1 cm)
Collection Jack Lenor Larsen

OPPOSITE
82. Jack Lenor Larsen
Academia, 1973
Wool, metallic gimp; double twill weave
Ireland
Montreal Museum of Fine Arts, The Liliane and David M. Stewart
Collection, Gift of Jack Lenor Larsen

The Larsen Studio has sustained relationships with mills all
over the world, including several in Ireland, where *Academia*
was made. Its highly sculptural effect took considerable time
to perfect and was finally achieved by the precise use of tightly
wrapped, paired metal yarns and a slubby worsted yarn interlaced in a double-woven twill construction. In the spirit of
the late nineteenth-century Arts and Crafts movement, Larsen
has always sought to escape the slick standardization of the
machine-made. His greatest early achievement was his ability
to produce the feel of the hand-made with power production.
The choice of distinctive yarns in generous quantity, sometimes
in rare constructions, served this end.

TOP RIGHT
83. Wayne Higby (American, b. 1943)
Lake Powell Memory—Labyrinth, 1996
Porcelain; hand-built, clear-glazed
17 x 20 x 11 in.
(43.2 x 50.7 x 28 cm)
East Hampton, New York, Collection LongHouse Reserve,
Gift of Helen W. Drutt English and Wayne Higby

FOLLOWING PAGES
84. Gwyn Hansen Piggott (Australian, b. 1935)
Echo #4 (six vessels), 1999
Limoges porcelain; wood-fired, glazed
Tallest 12 x 18½ x 7 in. (30.5 x 47 x 17.8 cm)
East Hampton, New York, Collection LongHouse Reserve,
Purchase, Larsen Fund

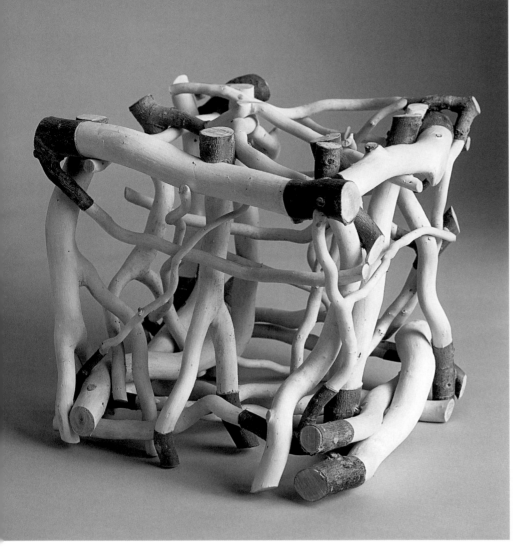

TOP LEFT
85. **Dorothy Gill Barnes** (American, b. 1927)
Corkscrew Willow Cube, 1999
Mulberry twigs; woven
8 x 8 x 8 in. (20.3 x 20.3 x 20.3 cm)
Collection Jack Lenor Larsen

BOTTOM LEFT
86. **Jiro Yonezawa** (Japanese, b. 1956)
Unexplored Regions, 1999
Bamboo, cane, cedar root, wood, urushi lacquer; interlaced
10 x 26 x 10⅝ in. (25.5 x 66 x 27 cm)
East Hampton, New York, Collection LongHouse Reserve,
Purchase, Larsen Fund

OPPOSITE
87. **Toshiko Takaezu** (American, b. 1929)
Closed Form, c. 1992
Glazed porcelain
7 x 6¼ x 6¼ in. (17.7 x 15.8 x 15.8 cm)
East Hampton, New York, Collection LongHouse Reserve,
Gift of Jack Lenor Larsen

88. **Helena Hernmarck**
(American, b. 1942)
Talking Trudeau-Nixon, 1969
Wool, nylon, linen; tapestry weave
Each panel 51 x 45 in.
(129.5 x 114.3 cm)
New York, Museum of Arts & Design, Gift of Jack Lenor Larsen
(panels 1 and 3); Collection Jack Lenor Larsen, promised gift to
Museum of Arts & Design (panel 2)

89. **Jack Lenor Larsen**
Triad, 1993
Cotton, rayon; jacquard double weave
United States
New York, Museum of Arts & Design, Gift of Cowtan & Tout

Ever since his university days, when he catalogued Pre-Columbian textiles, Larsen has been inspired by historic as well as ethnographic cloths. Unlike many textile designers, he has never succumbed to the temptation of simply replicating imagery. By taking the time to become familiar with diverse cultural aesthetics and techniques, the Larsen design team has produced fabric that takes full advantage of twentieth-century technology and aesthetics and, at the same time, honors the spirit of specific textile traditions. Sometimes entire collections embody this spirit, such as the African Collection of the mid-1960s and the Afghan Collection created in the 1970s, while at other times it is evident in individual pieces such as *Triad*.

Triad was inspired by patchwork bark cloth from the Republic of the Congo. For centuries, West and Central African peoples have been using the inner bark of certain trees to create a cloth to meet most of their everyday needs. The spirit of the roughly textured, pieced construction was captured by the studio and translated into a contemporary cloth. Highlighted by the contrast of the chenille and smooth yarns, the irregular triangular shapes of *Triad* are arranged in both the horizontal and the vertical axes and catch the jazzy, spontaneous spirit of the original cloth.

90. **Hans Coper** (British, b. Germany, 1920–1981)
Vessel (Cycladic Series), c. 1980
Stoneware; unglazed, burnished
12 x 2¾ x 1⅝ in. (30.5 x / x 4 cm)
East Hampton, New York, Collection LongHouse Reserve,
Gift of Jack Lenor Larsen

91. **Linda Bills** (American, b. 1943)
Japanese Armor, 1985
Wood; bent, pegged
12¾ x 26⅝ x 11¾ in. (32.4 x 67.6 x 29.9 cm)
Collection Jack Lenor Larsen

92. **Rudy Autio** (American, b. 1926)
Drum Lummond Ladies and Lippizano, c. 1983
Stoneware; hand-built, glazed
29¾ x 16⅛ x 14⅛ in. (75.5 x 41 x 36 cm)
Collection Jack Lenor Larsen

93. **Richard Devore** (American, b. 1933)
Torso, c. 1974
Stoneware; hand-built
12 x 10 x 11 in. (30.5 x 25.4 x 27.9 cm)
East Hampton, New York, Collection LongHouse Reserve,
Gift of Jack Lenor Larsen

ABOVE
94. Unknown artist, Thailand
Vessel, *c.* 2500 BCE
Pottery, coiled, honed
22½ x 18 x 18 in. (57.1 x 45.7 x 45.7 cm)
Collection Jack Lenor Larsen

OPPOSITE
95. Richard Landis (American, b. 1931)
Hanging, 1976 (detail)
Polyester and linen; double plain weave, cotton stitching
18 x 13 in. (45.7 x 33 cm)
Collection Jack Lenor Larsen

FOLLOWING PAGES
96. Jack Lenor Larsen
Landis II, 1982
Worsted; double plain weave
New Zealand
East Hampton, New York, Collection LongHouse Reserve

Richard Landis, an artist-weaver from Arizona, wove the original double-cloth composition for this fabric. It is striped in warp and weft with eight colors against a solid matrix to achieve a total of sixty-four color possibilities. Larsen adapted the pattern for upholstery and composed the reverse "plaid" side (p. 149) to create two distinct patterns in one cloth.

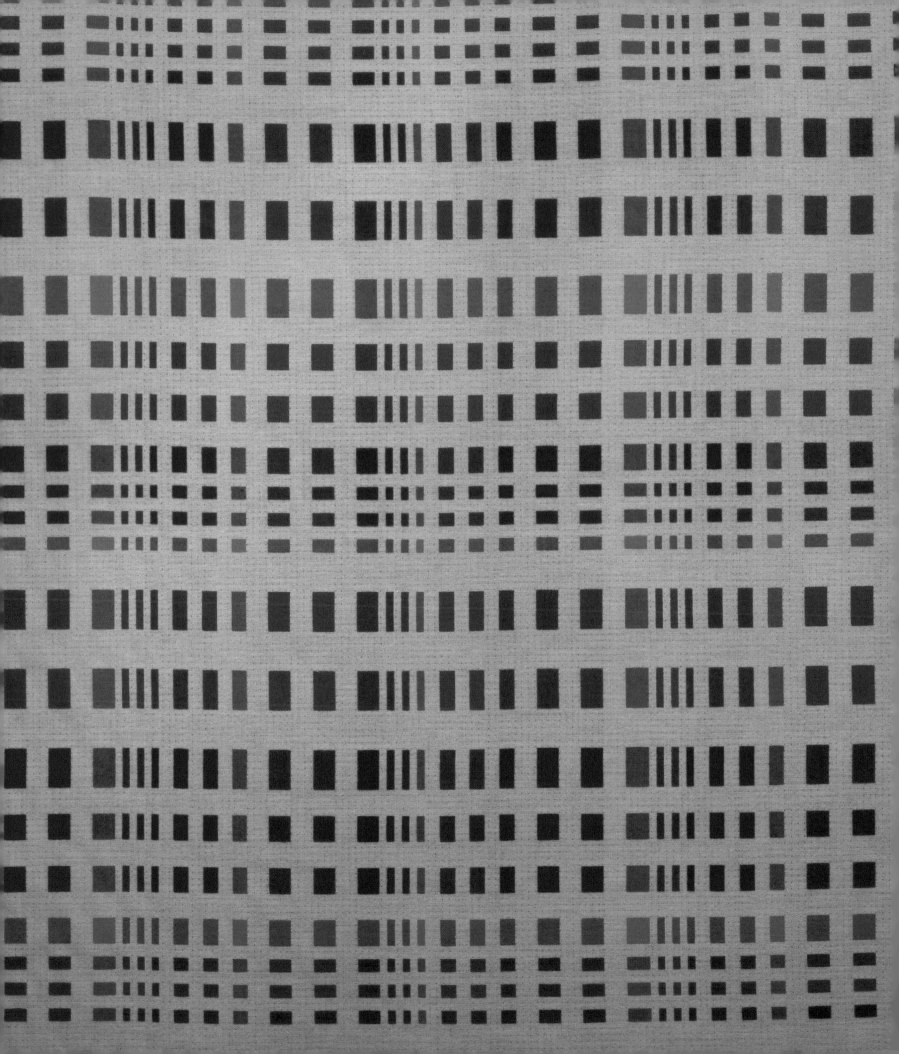

97. Jack Lenor Larsen
Mercury, 1969
Verel, metallic glimp, rayon, cotton; leno weave
United States
New York, Collection Cowtan & Tout

Some textiles produced by the company were initially developed in response to a specific commission. These commissions frequently had special requirements such as abrasion- and fire-resistance. In addition, fabrics created for airliners often had weight restrictions. *Mercury*, which was used for cabin dividers in Braniff airplanes, was a particular challenge in this respect because of its weighty metal yarn. The problem was overcome through the use of a leno construction that created very small yet stable spaces between warp and weft elements, and therefore required less metal yarn.

Win Anderson, head of the Design Studio from 1953 to 1976, remembers that the fabric was a bronze color, but when introduced as part of the Larsen line, it was only available in Molten Silver.

98. Chunghi Choo (Korean, b. 1938)
Lily Vase, 1980
Copper, silver plate; electro-formed
23 x 3⅝ x 4 in. (58.4 x 9.2 x 10.2 cm)
Collection Jack Lenor Larsen

ABOVE

99. **Richard Devore** (American, b. 1938)

Vessel, 1970s

Stoneware; hand-built, glazed

2 x 9⅝ x 9⅝ in. (5 x 24.6 x 24.6 cm)

East Hampton, New York, Collection LongHouse Reserve,

Gift of Jack Lenor Larsen

OPPOSITE

100. **Unknown artist**, Japan

Vessel, Jomon culture, 1500–1400 BCE

Ceramic; hand-built

23⅝ x 15 x 15 in. (60 x 38.1 x 38.1 cm)

East Hampton, New York, Collection LongHouse Reserve,

Purchase, Larsen Fund

101. **Unknown artist,** Tutsi people, Burunda
Milk jug, *c.* 1990
Hardwood; turned, honed
19 x 7½ x 7½ in.
(48.3 x 19.1 x 19.1 cm)
Collection Jack Lenor Larsen

RIGHT AND FOLLOWING PAGES
102. **Jack Lenor Larsen**
Architecture, c. 1965
Cotton; jacquard-woven terrycloth
Licensed to J.P. Stevens
United States
Collection Jack Lenor Larsen

In addition to the designs made for its own brand, the Larsen
Studio has always designed for other manufacturers. This has
sometimes involved commissions or consultations, but more
often the work resulted in collections developed under a
licensing agreement using the Larsen name. In 1963 the studio
created the first designer towel collection, for J.P. Stevens,
at that time the world's second largest textile manufacturer.
Jacquard towels were new then as well, and perhaps never
before designed by weavers who understood the potential
of two-sided, yarn-dyed terrycloth. Larsen observed that each
side of the fabric could be a different color: one side striped
and the other solid. With jacquard weaving, these two sides
could also be combined, even integrated, for pointillist-like
tweeds. As Stevens was new to towel production, the Larsen
Studio proposed an extremely bold collection that could not
go unnoticed. It was introduced like exotic couture, and it
became a best-selling American towel line. *Architecture*, from
the second collection for J.P. Stevens, is even more complex
than the first, with sculptural voids and Italian hill-town motifs.

103. **Steve Heineman** (Canadian, b. 1957)
Bowl, c. 1990
Stoneware, hand-built
4 x 9¾ x 6½ in. (10 x 25 x 16.5 cm)
Collection Jack Lenor Larsen

104. **Unknown artist**, Philippines
Baskets (set of three), twentieth century
Bamboo; interlaced
left to right:
6¼ x 3⅛ x 3⅛ in. (16 x 8 x 8 cm)
9¾ x 5⅛ x 5⅛ in. (25 x 13 x 13 cm);
5½ x 3¾ x 3¾ in. (14 x 9.5 x 9.5 cm);
Collection Jack Lenor Larsen

105. **Judy Kensley McKie** (American, b. 1943)
Lion Bench, 1994
Bronze; cast
17 x 72½ x 17 in. (43.2 x 183.9 x 43.2 cm)
East Hampton, New York, Collection LongHouse Reserve,
partial gift, the artist and Pritam & Eames Gallery, and partial
purchase, Larsen Fund

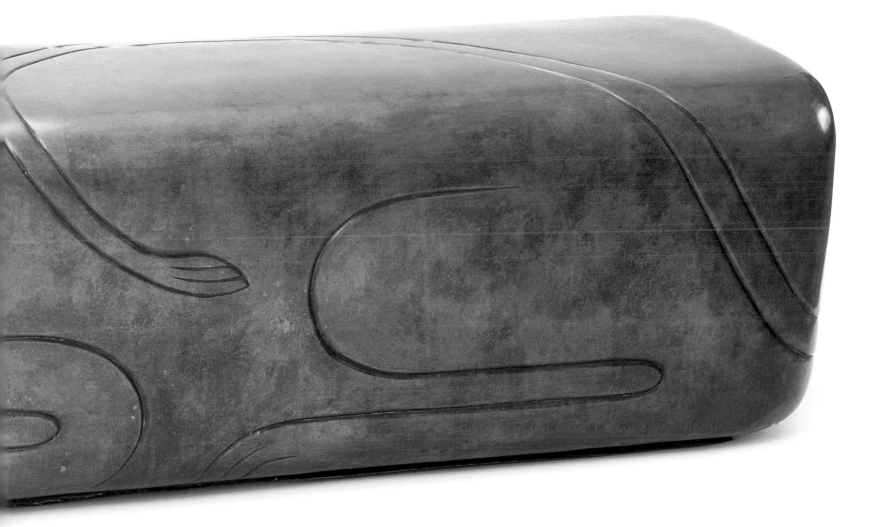

Context and Commissions

106. Jack Lenor Larsen
Three mock-up seats for Braniff Airlines, 1969,
made for Larsen's 1979–80 exhibition at the Louvre, Paris
Worsted; damask weave
Each 34⅝ x 20 x 34⅝ in. (88 x 51 x 88 cm)
Montreal Museum of Fine Arts,
The Liliane and David M. Stewart Collection,
Gift of Jack Lenor Larsen

107. Jack Lenor Larsen
Hanging, c. 1954 (detail)
Dune-grass roots, cotton linen; woven
43 x 13⅜ in. (109 x 34 cm)
Collection Jack Lenor Larsen

OPPOSITE
108. Jack Lenor Larsen
Curtain fragment from the Filene Center Theater,
Wolftrap Farm, near Washington, D.C., 1972
Woven; mohair, nylon
East Hampton, New York, Collection LongHouse Reserve

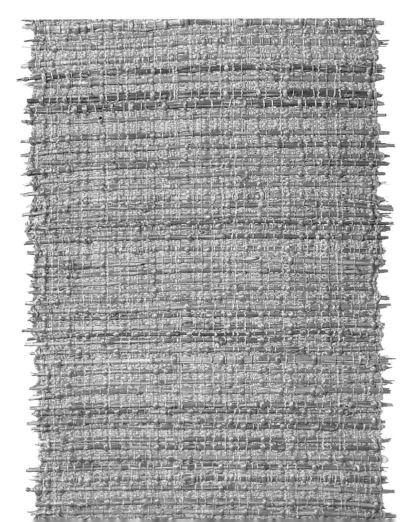

110. **Jack Lenor Larsen**
Three neckties, c. 1951
Mixed fibers; hand-woven
Longest 50 in. (127 cm)
Collection Jack Lenor Larsen

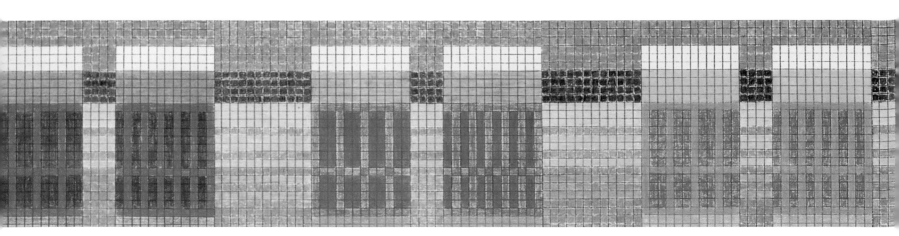

111. **Jack Lenor Larsen**
Rendering of the lobby hanging for Sears Bank & Trust, Chicago,
1974–75, designed by Skidmore, Owings & Merrill
Watercolor on paper; 11½ x 35½ in. (29 x 90 cm)
Collection Jack Lenor Larsen

112. **Jack Lenor Larsen**
Screen, c. 1951
Wood, redwood, fiber, jute, cotton; woven
69 x 83 in. (175.8 x 211.2 cm) (full length)
Montreal Museum of Fine Arts, The Liliane and David M. Stewart
Collection, Gift of Jack Lenor Larsen

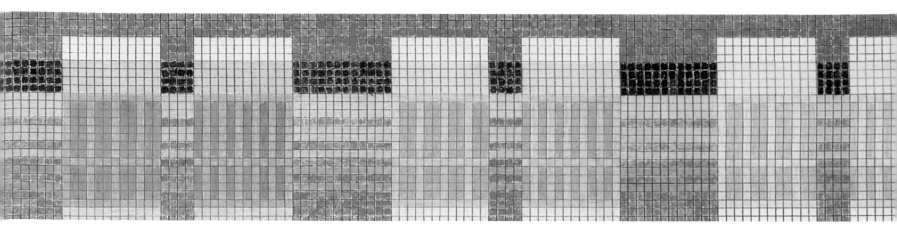

Chronology
compiled by Anne Hoy

1927

Born August 5 in Seattle, to Mabel Larsen (1903–1998) and Elmer Lenor Larsen (1902–1980), who came from Alberta, Canada, and traced their ancestry to Norway and Denmark. Jack, an only child, later writes: "If I once envied painters their being able to work independently of colleagues and suppliers, I learned that the studio and larger Larsen organization were unknowingly created as an extended family, in which I would be both followed and looked after. . . . What I have achieved was never accomplished alone."[1]

1933

The family moves to Bremerton, across Puget Sound, where Jack's father, a building contractor, is constructing a waterfront home. Through the 1930s a family friend and a teacher encourage Larsen's interest in world geography, history,

and design. In 1939 the Larsens move into a house filled with a decade of subscriptions to *Vanity Fair*, *House & Garden*, and *Vogue*, as well as publications on Frank Lloyd Wright.

1945

Enrolls in the School of Architecture at the University of Washington, Seattle, where the students had included architect Minoru Yamasaki and furniture maker George Nakashima. In the Northwest, "the Japanese [design] influence was very strong . . . [with] a sensitivity to wood finishes and to understatement, to low-key colors and to hand craft. . . . It was a cultural aesthetic we . . . thought was new, free, and liberating—as opposed to European traditions. . . . The intimacy of scale and the simplicity of style associated with Japan seemed to suit our democratic lifestyle."[2]

1946–47

Larsen studies interior and furniture design under Hope Foote in the art department, lifestyle subjects with Margaret Hosmer,[3] and textiles under Grace Denny, learning fibers, structure, finishes, testing, use, and care. When an aristocratic Peruvian-born friend, Chan Khan, introduces him to Pre-Columbian fabrics and ceramics, he acquires the examples he can afford, in addition to Northwest Coast Indian basketry. "Then, as now, the characteristic common to my acquisitions was not luxury, nor even quality in a usual sense, but their existing outside the conventions I knew."[4]

1947

Fall, moves to Los Angeles to concentrate on fabric; enrolls in University of Southern California's School of Architecture.

Remoulade, 1956

1948

Spring, studies philosophy and modern art at USC; determines to be a weaver. At Dorothea Hulse's Handcraft House in Los Angeles, a custom-weave shop and school, he teaches modern color and design while learning weaving there —a dual commitment to design practice and pedagogy that will continue. About being an instructor at age twenty-one, Larsen observes that "modern design and color were so new that not many were available to teach."[5] Fall, returns to University of Washington and takes graduate seminars in cultural anthropology.

1949–50

For Grace Denny at the University of Washington, who is then translating Raoul d'Harcourt's *The Textiles of Ancient Peru and Their Techniques* (French edn. 1933), he analyses textile structures and makes diagrammatic reconstructions. He also becomes assistant to Ed Rossbach, who is teaching weaving after completing his MFA at the famed applied arts school the Cranbrook Academy of Art. Larsen's job teaching for the Seattle Weavers' Guild leads him to direct further weaving courses, while he opens his own weaving studio near campus. "In these post-war years [1945–50] . . . Beaux-Arts architecture caved in to Modernism. . . . Northwest houses, individually designed and furnished by our regional architects [notably Pietro Belluschi, John Yeon, and Roland Terry], demanded new cloths unavailable through commercial fabric manufacturers. To express the materials and structure of their making . . . called for custom-designed, hand-woven cloths. . . . Commissions came as quickly as they could be woven." First solo exhibition in 1949, at Portland's Contemporary Crafts Association (then the Oregon Ceramic Studio), said to be the oldest craft gallery in US. Larsen graduates from the University of Washington

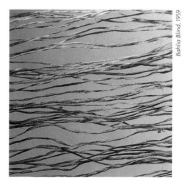

Bahlia Blind, 1959

175

with a special degree: general studies with a concentration in textiles—a field in which the university offered no degree.

1950

Fall, with recommendations from Rossbach and a scholarship, Larsen begins the MFA program at Cranbrook, architect Eliel Saarinen's elite graduate school of art, architecture, and design in Bloomfield Hills, Michigan. Fabric designer Marianne Strengell, his "weave master," who was widely known for her plays of texture in somber Finnish monochromes, is startled by what she calls his "California colors"—a palette of coral, Spanish orange, turquoise, and bronzed green. She proclaims, Larsen recalls, that "as I was the scholarship student, she expected double the quantity as well as the quality of the others." The speed and organization this required "served me well in the start-up years of my company." His graduate degree exhibition includes a large screen woven of yarns and redwood slats on a rug loom (pl. 112).

1951

Armed with the Cranbrook degree, which he earned in two semesters, and introductions from such clients as Lydia Winston, daughter of architect Albert Kahn, Larsen is invited to work in New York by Thaibok Ltd., the importer of Jim Thompson's Thai silks, and by Arundell Clarke, former first director of Knoll Textiles, who gives him studio space. Recommended by Clarke and the Raymond Loewy design firm, he weaves lobby draperies for Lever House designed by Skidmore, Owings & Merrill—

among America's first International Style office towers. He also weaves window treatments for furniture designer Edward Wormley. For his first collection for Thaibok, he hires Richard Bolan, who had "extraordinary skills enabling him to 'handweave' on power looms."

Together Larsen and Bolan "learned to power weave more and more complex assemblages of exotic yarns. Craftsmanship and ingenuity, I soon learned, were not limited to hand-weaving, nor did they require art-school training." Larsen's power-woven fabrics with the look of hand-weaves, such as *Granite*, become a widespread market influence. His work is part of the 1951–55 *Good Design* exhibitions at the Museum of Modern Art: influential annuals organized by Edgar Kaufmann, Jr., in collaboration with Chicago's Merchandise Mart, to showcase worthy, commercially available products and prototypes by contemporary designers. His sample weaves tailored as neckties (pl. 110) lead to commissions from high-end men's clothing stores in Manhattan.

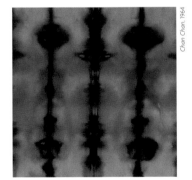

Chan Chan, 1964

1952

Establishes Jack Lenor Larsen, incorporated [*sic*]. Cranbrook classmate Win Anderson and Bob Carr, both weavers, join the firm by 1954,

and Manning Field becomes business manager. Larsen credits a trip to Haiti in 1952 with beginning what will become a lifelong, global involvement with native fabric techniques and hand-spun yarns. He imports the first hand-spun, hand-woven fabrics from Haiti, then others from Morocco, Colombia, and Mexico, countries in which he adapts local hand-spun, hand-woven cloths for import to the US. "In no case did I really develop the production capability," Larsen later recalls. "What I did was to work on design and coloring and, in some cases, improve the technology, such as better dyes for the Haitian and Mexican weavers."[6]

He is becoming known as "the natural fiber man." In new offices and homes, his fabrics' "organic variations in texture and color became the perfect antidote for monotonous surfaces of laminate and drywall." Meanwhile industrial popularization of his olives and ochres will "become the Avocado and Harvest Gold color epidemic" of the early 1960s. From 1952 to 1972, is a guest writer for *Craft Horizons* magazine. Starting in 1952, he teaches for thirteen consecutive summers at Haystack Mountain School of Crafts in Maine, where he soon chooses the faculty and joins the board.

1953–65

Designs and produces fabric for such fashion designers as Pauline Trigère, Donald Brooks, B.H. Wragge, and Jax of California. For two seasons, designs women's and men's apparel under his own J.L. Arbiter label, introducing the first down-filled coat to fashion; and in 1963 also offers a modestly priced apparel fabrics line, Ja-El Fabrics.

Architecture, 1965

1954

Opens the first Larsen showroom, at Park Avenue and 58th Street; shows his first collection, Spice Garden, including romantic hand-prints that establish him in patterned cloths. This decorative line, inspired by Tiffany and Matisse, succeeds with both Modernists and conservatives. Begins producing hand-spun and hand-woven upholsteries in Morocco. On the inaugural design tour of Europe organized by the American Institute of Designers, he visits Italy and France for first time. While designing custom hangings for corporate headquarters, he creates more affordable works for average wallets, such as a hanging of dune-grass roots and linen (pl. 107).

Samarkand, 1967

1955

Invited to join board of the new American Craft Council, and helps lay cornerstone of the Museum of Arts & Design (then the Museum of Contemporary Crafts and subsequently the American Craft Museum), New York.

1956

Exhibition of his work at M.H. De Young Museum, San Francisco. For three years, in the mid-1950s, he designs mostly printed collections for Charles Bloom, the large fabric converter. A Macy's commission to Bloom for a Larsen collection of color-coordinated prints becomes the store's best-selling introduction in twenty years, "a flower garden of vibrating modern color—not hesitant or accommodating, but a fresh breakthrough in a period when fabrics were still of major importance to department stores."

1957

As guest editor for *Interiors* magazine, reports on 11th Milan Triennial (and on those of 1961 and 1964) and buys heavily from this international design exhibition, including the entire exhibit from Sardinia. Edited by Olga Gueft, the magazine was then "documenting the fever pitch of the Modern Movement . . . on both sides of the Atlantic."

1958

Opens Larsen Design Studio (also known as Larsen Design Corporation), with Win Anderson as president, for consultation to industry, development of new fibers, yarns, and coloring, and large-scale architectural projects. Designs fabrics for Pan American's 707 jet fleet, the first jet airliners. Joins the team of industrial designer Russel Wright, a consultant to US State Department, to design exports crafted in Taiwan and South Vietnam.

1958–59

Takes first of eight trips to South America; in Peru, researches for his Andean Collection; in Brazil, does research for fabrics commissioned by Varig Airlines and by the architects of Brasilia, the new capital city. Designs what is believed to be the first diagonal-stripe weave and the first American hand-screens on velvet: "If it seemed curious then that a weaver would become best known for sumptuous hand-prints, the commonality was color expression: my quest from the '60s was to bring the effulgence of country gardens indoors, into cities."[7]

As board member and chair of building committee at Haystack Mountain School of Crafts, he selects Edward Larrabee Barnes as architect of Deer Isle campus. Until 1962 is co-director of Fabric Design Department at the Philadelphia College of Art.

Oberon, 1969

1959–60

With Russel Wright's team, travels to Taiwan and South Vietnam to research grass weaving; also stops off in Japan. In South Vietnam, weaves seagrass carpets with refugee weavers from Hanoi. In Bangkok he weekends with Jim Thompson, the American architect who revived silk weaving there at end of World War II and established the Thai Silk Company, which supplied for World Crafts Congress, visits Himalayan kingdom of Sikkim at invitation of Hope Cooke, its ruler's American wife. After Nixon's historic trip to China, Larsen is invited there to survey export potential for Chinese silks. Is asked back four more times, to Canton, Beijing, and Manchuria, in 1973–76; begins producing tussah upholsteries in Manchuria.

Luxor, 1980

1974–75

In New Zealand for International Wool Bureau, researches Maori fabrics and makes contact with upholstery and carpet weavers. Designs *Visiona IV* exhibition in Frankfurt for Bayer AG; installs twenty-eight quilted silk hangings for main floor of Sears Bank & Trust, Chicago, then tallest building in world, on commission from architects Skidmore, Owings & Merrill (illus. on p. 167).

1975

Artist in Residence, Royal College of Art, London. Advisory Council, Museum of Modern Art, New York, through 1996. Publishes *Fabric for Interiors: A Guide for Architects, Designers, and Consumers*, with Jeanne Weeks (New York: Van Nostrand Reinhold).

1976

Exhibition at Kunstindustrietmuseum, Copenhagen. Establishes Larsen Furniture division, completing his offerings for total interior design.

1977

Guest curator of *Wall Hangings: The New Classicism* exhibition, Museum of Modern Art, New York.

1978

Theater curtain for St. Charles, Illinois, Cultural Center. Retrospective entitled *The Larsen Influence: The First 25 Years* at Fashion Institute of Technology, New York. Made Honorary Fellow, American Society of Interior Designers; Fellow, American Craft Council; and Eliot Noyes Fellow of the Aspen International Design Conference. Given honorary title of affiliate professor by University of Washington.

In Japan, stays in Kyoto "to focus on traditional Japan" while he designs for porcelain factories of Nagoya, where Dansk and later Mikasa will manufacture his dinnerware (his Tapestries tableware for Dansk, 1980, is one of its continued best-sellers). In Japan, which "continues to be my favorite country . . . thought races forward. The optimum is not dismissed as an impossibility. Superb quality is still a norm. . . . Asian

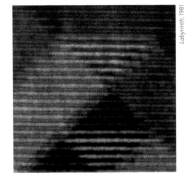

Labyrinth, 1981

achievers travel and observe to become more cosmopolitan, perhaps because they escape the parochial limits of New Yorkers or Parisians, who think they are at the center." He has traveled almost annually to Japan since 1959 and continues to do so.

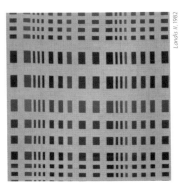

Lordis II, 1982

1979–80

Retrospective, *Jack Lenor Larsen: 30 Years of Creative Textiles*, is second exhibition to be devoted to an American, after Mark Tobey, at Musée des Arts Décoratifs, Palais du Louvre, Paris. In catalogue, the curator Françoise Mathey writes, "Jack Lenor Larsen could have become a sculptor, a painter, or a poet, but he chose to be a weaver because, through textiles, he could be a painter, architect, and poet all at once. . . . We recognize the craftsman by his masterpiece. Larsen, however, is an artist because, instead of a single masterpiece, he prefers a long-term and harmonious work that continues to search and evolve." Awarded honorary doctorate by Parsons School of Design, New School of Social Research, New York.

1981–90

President, American Craft Council; during tenure, co-chairs building committee for new museum on 53rd Street, New York.

1981

Co-director of *The Art Fabric: Mainstream*, traveling exhibition opening at Museum of Modern Art, San Francisco. Publishes *The Art Fabric: Mainstream* with Mildred Constantine (New York: Van Nostrand Reinhold).

1982

Awarded honorary doctorate of fine arts, Rhode Island School of Design.

1983

Named Honorary RDI (Royal Designer for Industry) by Royal Society of Arts, London.

1983–84

Contributor to *Design Since 1945* exhibition and author of essay on textiles in book of same name, Philadelphia Museum of Art.

Carnival, 1937

1985

Drawing on Navajo, Inca, and Inuit motifs, designs Terra Nova Collection, including textiles, wall coverings, rugs, and domestics, for manufacturers Mikasa, Martex, et al., to help support Museum of American Indian.

1986

Curator of *Interlacing: The Elemental Fabric*, traveling exhibition opening at Textile Museum, Washington, D.C.

Author of book-catalogue, with Betty Freudenheim. Curator of *Splendid Forms*, on subject of craft media, Bellas Artes Gallery, Santa Fe, New Mexico. "I have a great many restrictions on what I can do, and to further the work of people without the same restrictions becomes all the more appealing." [11]

1988

Curator of traveling exhibition and author of catalogue *The Tactile Vessel: New Basket Forms* (Erie Art Museum, Pennsylvania), on the collection he formed for this small museum. Author of *Material Wealth: Living with Luxurious Fabrics* (New York and London: Abbeville and Thames & Hudson).

1990

Elected President Emeritus, American Craft Council.

1991

Establishes LongHouse Foundation (now LongHouse Reserve) as a non-profit public educational organization at his residence in East Hampton, New York, which is designed in collaboration with architect Charles Forberg on the model of the seventh-century Shinto shrine of Ise in Japan. Open to public from May through mid-September, this sixteen-acre estate, with gallery, arboretum, and sculpture gardens, continues to host performing arts events and changing exhibitions of fine and applied arts (illus. on pp. 8, 11).

1992

Receives Roscoe Award from *Interior Design* magazine, and Founder's Medal from Cranbrook Academy of

Art. Designs carpets, wall and window fabrics, leather upholstery for Trustees' Dining Room, Metropolitan Museum of Art, New York.

1993

Receives Brooklyn Museum Design Award for Lifetime Achievement.

Hologram Leaves, 1990

1996

Awarded Gold Medal by American Craft Council; Textile Design Institute Medal; Lifetime Achievement Award by the Surface Design organization. Arranges for installation of glass by Dale Chihuly at LongHouse, the artist's first environmental work created for landscape.

1997

Merger of Larsen company with Cowtan & Tout, the US subsidiary of London-based Colefax & Fowler Group; remains as consultant and continues to develop new designs. Colefax & Fowler donate Larsen archive to collaborating institutions in Minnesota: the Minneapolis Institute of Arts, the University of Minnesota's Goldstein Museum of Design, and the university's Elmer L. Andersen Library. Three exhibitions based on the gift open in late 2001; the Minneapolis Institute of Arts show travels to two US museums in 2002–03.

Mimosa Sheer, 1990

1998

Publishes *Jack Lenor Larsen: A Weaver's Memoir* (New York: Harry N. Abrams; reissued in paperback 2003).

1999

Design Arts Award from Montreal Museum of Decorative Arts.

2000

Lifetime Achievement Award, American Craft Museum; Hall of Fame Award, Whitney Publications, New York.

Cumulus, 1991

2001

Honorary doctorate of fine arts, New York School of Interior Design.

2002

Celebrates his seventy-fifth birthday at LongHouse at a benefit for the institution. It has permanent and long-term installations of art by Isamu Noguchi, Alfonso Ossorio, Dale Chihuly, and Toshiko Takeazu, among others. LongHouse Reserve was established, he writes, "as a case study to exemplify a creative approach to contemporary lifestyle, with the full belief that the visitor experiencing art in a living space has a learning experience far removed from the commercial priorities of model rooms or show houses."[12] The mission of LongHouse is "to exemplify living with art in all forms. . . . [It] brings together art and nature, aesthetics and spirit, with a strong conviction that the arts are central to living wholly and creatively. Dedicated to quality and integrity, LongHouse programs encourage a broad concept of learning."[13]

Onward!, 1997

2003

Award from Rhode Island School of Design and Honorary Doctorate from Royal College of Art, London. Lifetime Award, Aid to Artisans, an organization that grew out of the World Craft Council and assists handcraft production in twenty countries.

[1] Quotations from Jack Larsen in this Chronology, unless otherwise noted, come from *Jack Lenor Larsen: A Weaver's Memoir*, New York (Harry N. Abrams) 1998; reissued 2003.

[2] Jack Lenor Larsen, as quoted in Jane Van Cleve, "Beyond Craft: Jack Lenor Larsen," *Stepping Out Northwest*, Spring 1982, p. 37.

[3] Larsen recalls the flamboyant Hosmer as giving conservative co-eds "lesson no. l, how to get rid of your hope chest, and lesson no. 2, how to get rid of the boy you were pinned to." Conversation with David A. Hanks office, January 14, 2003.

[4] Conversation with David A. Hanks office, January 14, 2003.

[5] Correspondence between Jack Lenor Larsen and David A. Hanks office, August 2002.

[6] *Ibid.*

[7] Jack Lenor Larsen, "A Reflective Glance," *Jack Lenor Larsen Retrospektive*, exhib. cat., Krefeld (Germany), Deutsches Textilmuseum, 1995, p. 9.

[8] Jack Lenor Larsen, "Fabrics in a New Dimension," *Industrial Design*, 9, no. 12 (December 1962), p. 90. The Endless House was Frederick Kiesler's conception of an organically shaped shelter.

[9] J. Simpson, "Jack Lenor Larsen— A Structural Approach to Fabric," *Architectural Digest*, April 1984, pp. 226, 230–32.

[10] Larsen, "A Reflective Glance," p. 9.

[11] Jack Lenor Larsen, as quoted in Van Cleve, "Beyond Craft: Jack Lenor Larsen," p. 42.

[12] Statement on LongHouse website, August 2002; www.longhouse.org.

[13] *LongHouse Reserve Newsletter*, 3, 2002, p. 2.

The Larsen Archives in Minnesota and Montreal
Lotus Stack

There is no substitute for original objects and written records, on which virtually all aspects of contemporary civilization are based. Archives are the collective memory of the institutions of the modern world and thus form an important part of our cultural heritage.

Alan Lathrop[1]

Throughout the twentieth century, Minnesota's fine arts and educational institutions have maintained a strong commitment to contemporary design. Thus, it was no surprise that the Jack Lenor Larsen company archives were brought to Minnesota in 1998, shortly after the firm was sold to Cowtan & Tout, the American subsidiary of Colefax & Fowler. Due to its size—over 25,000 items—no one institution in the state had the capacity to house this valuable resource in its entirety. Therefore the objects and records were divided between the Minneapolis Institute of Arts and the University of Minnesota. In addition to the original gift, the archive has been supplemented by twenty tape-recorded interviews with former Larsen employees and business associates who played a significant part in the company's contribution to twentieth-century design.

Win Anderson, who was with the company from 1953 to 1976 and served as Larsen Design Studio's first president, initiated a policy of preserving representative samples of all Larsen textiles and maintained the early company records. The pressures of running a company did not always permit consistent record-keeping, however, and the archived materials vary dramatically in size and quality. The archive is most complete in objects and related information for the first half of the company's history, from the late 1950s through the 1970s. Sometimes, if a design sold out, no example remained, while at other times, only a rejected production trial represents a specific pattern or color variation. The few less-than-perfect samples in this collection illustrate the various challenges the company faced as it worked to produce its innovative designs. These objects tell stories of technical refinements, problem-solving, and even detours, as some designs were judged unviable.

The majority of Larsen Design Studio production yardage samples are stored at the Minneapolis Institute of Arts. Additional colorways of many of these designs are housed at the Goldstein Museum of Design at the University of Minnesota. The Goldstein also holds the extant examples of licensed production created by the studio. Most of the archive's business records came from the purchasing and production division, directed for many years by Bob Carr, a vice-president of the company. These records, along with original drawings and artwork on paper, are housed in the Northwest Architectural Archive at the university.

Scholars of textile history, designers, students, and admirers of Jack Lenor Larsen and Larsen Design Studio are indebted to Mr. Larsen, to Cowtan & Tout, and to Colefax & Fowler for facilitating this significant gift.

For access to the growing database of Larsen material at the Minneapolis Institute of Arts, consult the interactive site Larsen: A Living Archive, http:www.artsmia.org/Larsen. Fabrics cited but not illustrated in this book can be seen at this site. The archive can be searched by decade, theme, or keyword.[2]

In 1999, Jack Larsen donated an archive of 819 of his textiles to the Montreal Museum of Decorative Arts, as part of the Liliane and David M. Stewart Collection. When the Stewart Collection was transferred to the Montreal Museum of Fine Arts in 2000, the Larsen archive was transferred as well. The archive also contains the contents of the exhibition *Jack Lenor Larsen: 30 Years of Creative Textiles*, which was organized by the Musée des Arts Décoratifs and exhibited at the Palais du Louvre in 1981. This includes the panels of fabric designed for the exhibition installation, as well as the chair mock-ups displaying Larsen's textile designs for Braniff Airlines.

Prior to Jack Larsen's donation of the archive and exhibition materials, the Montreal Museum of Decorative Arts had acquired a representative collection of textile lengths. They are now part of the Stewart Collection at the Montreal Museum of Fine Arts.

[1] Alan Lathrop is the curator of the Manuscripts Division of the University of Minnesota Libraries.

[2] The Larsen website was created in conjunction with the exhibition of 2001, *Jack Lenor Larsen: The Company and the Cloth*, at the Minneapolis Institute of Arts. At the same time the University of Minnesota published *Interplay: Perspectives on the Design Legacy of Jack Lenor Larsen*, ed. Denise Guerin and Stephanie Watson, with essays by Alan Lathrop, Krista Stack Pawar, Lindsay Shen, Lotus Stack, and Stephanie Watson, Minneapolis MN (Goldstein Museum of Design/University of Minnesota) 2001.

Glossary

batik
A resist pattern in which liquid such as wax is drawn or blocked onto a fabric before dyeing.

block printing
General term for a hand-printing process using wood, metal, or linoleum blocks into which patterns have been made.

bobbin or Nottingham lace
A single set-of-elements construction, originally hand-made on a pillow with numerous yarns.

burn-out, etching, or *devoré* printing
A printing process in which an opaque or translucent pattern is produced by applying acid to areas of a fabric, usually made of a fiber separate from the ground cloth.

casement or casement cloth
A general term for sheer drapery fabric.

chevron
A herringbone weave in a zigzag pattern.

colorway
One individual coloration for the full color line.

damask
A woven pattern based upon contrasting warp-face and filling-face areas.

devoré
See **burn-out printing**

dimensional stability
The degree to which a fabric will retain its original shape or size.

discharge printing
A printing process in which the pattern is bleached out of already dyed goods; it may be replaced with another color.

double cloth
A compound cloth based on two sets each of warp and filling held together at regular intervals by warp or filling yarns passing from one layer to the other.

filament
A continuous strand of silk or man-made fiber, also available in cut-filament, or staple, form. The diametric size of a filament is measured in deniers.

filling, weft or woof
An element carried horizontally on a shuttle through the open shed of the vertical warp in a woven fabric.

flame inhibitor
A functional finish, often applied in conjunction with other finishes and sold under a variety of trade names.

flame-resistant, or flame-retardant, fabric
A fabric whose fiber content or topical finish makes it difficult to ignite and slow to burn.

float
The portion of a warp or filling yarn that rides over two or more opposing yarns to form a sleek face, as in satin, or is grouped to form a pattern on the face, as in brocade.

gimp
Usually a silk or metallic yarn spiral-wrapped closely around an inner core to cover it completely.

hand-loomed
Woven on a fly-shuttle hand loom.

hand-printing process
A variety of preindustrial printing techniques that are done by hand, including resist, block, and hand-screen prints.

heat setting
A process in which fabrics of thermoplastic fibers are tentered under controlled heat to stabilize dimensions and to minimize future shrinkage or stretching.

herringbone
A twill weave that reverses direction across the fabric to form a chevron.

horsehair
A narrow upholstery fabric woven with a filling of long, single horsehairs.

honeycomb
A hexagonally patterned piqué weave.

ikat
A fabric woven with tie-dyed yarns.

jacquard
A pattern-controlling attachment for looms and knitting or lace machines.

kilim
A pileless tapestry-woven carpet, mat, or spread.

leno, or **marquisette**
A woven fabric construction in which two or more warp ends twist between insertions of weft.

Lurex
Trade name of a slit-film metallic yarn produced by Dow

Badische.moiré
A wavy, watered pattern produced in finishing.

monofilament
A yarn composed of a single untwisted and unplied synthetic filament.

nub
A random clot of short, dense fibers incorporated during spinning.

pile
A velvety surface produced by an extra set of warp or filling yarns that form raised loops, which may be cut and sheared or left uncut.

pile weave
A fabric with cut or uncut loops above the surface of the ground cloth, such as terrycloth, velvet, velour, plush, and many carpets.

plain weave
The simplest and most basic woven construction, in which one end (or **warp**) interlaces alternately with one pick (or **weft**).

plush
A pile-woven cloth with a higher and less dense pile than velvet or velour.

ramie
A fine bast fiber.

rep
A plain-woven fabric characterized by raised, rounded ribs, running from selvage to selvage.

Saran
Both a trade name and a generic term for a man-made fiber composed of at least 8% polymerized vinylidene chloride.

screen printing
A hand- or machine-printing process in which a pattern-making stencil or screen held in a frame is positioned on the cloth and colorant is applied.

sheer
A transparent or semi-opaque fabric.

slub
A heavy area in an unevenly spun yarn.

terrycloth
An uncut warp-pile fabric, plain- or jacquard-woven, usually of cotton, linen, or rayon.

thermoplastic fiber
A fiber that softens or fuses with heat and hardens again when cooled and so is capable of permanent memory.

transfer printing
A printing process in which a pattern is printed on waxed paper and transferred to the cloth under heat and pressure.

twill
A basic weave in which the filling yarns pass over and under warp yarns in successive progression to create the appearance of diagonal lines.

velvet
(1) A pile fabric with a short, soft, dense pile. (2) A woven fabric construction characterized by the insertion of an extra warp that is looped over wires and cut.

Verel
Trade name of a modern acrylic fiber produced by Eastman.

warp
A series of yarns extending lengthwise on a loom and running parallel to the selvage.

warp knit
(1) A fabric produced on a knitting machine in which the yarns run in a lengthwise but zigzag direction, producing excellent stability in a vertical direction. (2) A tricot knit.

warp print
A pattern printed on the warp prior to weaving, which results in an indistinct image.

weft or **woof**
See **filling**

worsted system
A spinning process by which long wool fibers are carded, combed, and spun into a smooth, compact yarn with average-to-high twist.

woven-double fabric
A velvet or plush fabric in which two ground cloths are woven one over the other, with the pile yarns woven up and down between them.

yarn dyeing
dyeing at the yarn stage of the production continuum rather than stock, solution, or piece dyeing.

This glossary is excerpted from *Jack Lenor Larsen, Fabrics for Interiors: A Guide for Architects, Designers, and Consumers* (copyright John Wiley & Sons, 1975), by permission of the publisher.

Index

Page numbers in *italics* refer to captions

Photographic Credits

First published 2004 by Merrell Publishers Limited

Head office
42 Southwark Street
London SE1 1UN

New York office
49 West 24th Street
New York, NY 10010

www.merrellpublishers.com

in association with

Museum of Arts & Design
40 West 53rd Street
New York, NY 10019
www.madmuseum.org

and

The Liliane and David M. Stewart Program for Modern
Design, Montreal

Published on the occasion of the exhibition *Jack Lenor
Larsen: Creator and Collector*, organized by the Museum
of Arts & Design, New York, and The Liliane and David M.
Stewart Program for Modern Design, Montreal

Exhibition itinerary:
Museum of Arts & Design, New York
Allentown Art Museum, Allentown, Pennsylvania
Musée d'Art Contemporain de Montréal, Quebec

This exhibition was made possible with the generous
support of Hunter Douglas and Cowtan & Tout.
Additional support was provided by The Coby
Foundation, Ltd., in honor of The Bank of New York,
the Helena Rubinstein Foundation, and the Roy and Niuta
Titus Foundation.

British Library Cataloguing-in-Publication Data:

McFadden, David
Jack Lenor Larsen : creator and collector
1.Larsen, Jack Lenor – Exhibitions 2.Larsen, Jack Lenor –
Art collections – Exhibitions 3.Art – Private collections –
United States – Exhibitions
I.Title II.Stack, Lotus III.Larsen, Jack Lenor IV.Museum of
Arts and Design (New York, N.Y.) V.Liliane and David M.
Stewart Program for Modern Design
746'.092

ISBN 1 85894 217 9 (hardback)
ISBN 1 85894 218 7 (paperback)

Edited by Anne H. Hoy
Produced by Merrell Publishers
Designed by Helen Taylor
Copy-edited by Jane Birkett
Indexed by Diana Lecore
Printed and bound in China

Front jacket/cover: Jack Lenor Larsen, *Seascape Sheer* (see pl. 17)
p. 3: At LongHouse, a vitrine with sliding panels of Larsen fabric
pp. 4–5: Jack Lenor Larsen, *Carnival* (detail of pl. 49)
pp. 36–37: Jack Lenor Larsen, *Nimbus* (detail of pl. 8)